T0305438

Valuing Early Stage and Venture-Backed Companies

Valuing Early Stage and Venture-Backed Companies

NEIL J. BEATON,
CPA/ABV, CFA, ASA

WILEY

John Wiley & Sons, Inc.

Published by John Wiley & Sons, Inc., Hoboken, New Jersey.
Published simultaneously in Canada.

For general information on our other products and services or for technical support,
please contact our Customer Care Department within the United States at (800)
762-2974, outside the United States at (317) 572-3993 or fax (317) 572-4002.

Wiley also publishes its books in a variety of electronic formats. Some content that
appears in print may not be available in electronic books. For more information about
Wiley products, visit our Web site at www.wiley.com.

Library of Congress Cataloging-in-Publication Data

Beaton, Neil J.
    Valuing early stage and venture backed companies / Neil J. Beaton.
        p. cm.
    Includes bibliographical references and index.
    ISBN 978-0-470-43629-5 (cloth)
  1. New business enterprises–Valuation.   2. Small business–Valuation.
3. Private companies–Valuation.   4. Business enterprises–Valuation.   I. Title.
    HG4028.V3B28 2010
    658.15′5–dc22   2009038773

Printed in the United States of America

10 9 8 7 6 5 4 3

To my family—Jill, Luke, Alana, Evan, Henry and Emily—and my longtime business partner, Bob Duffy, without whose unwavering support and ability to put up with me, I could never have focused long enough to complete this book

Contents

Preface

Early stage company valuation is unique in the overall sphere of business valuation. Early stage companies often lack the traditional valuation metrics of cash flow, earnings, or even revenue at times. Without these metrics, traditional discounted cash flow models and comparison to public markets or private transactions take on less relevance, and a more "experiential" valuation approach is called for. Familiarity with the venture capital industry and its investment practices is critical to a well-reasoned early stage company valuation. In 2004, the American Institute of Certified Public Accountants published a practice aid known as *Valuation of Privately-Held-Company Equity Securities Issued as Compensation*. During the past five years, this practice aid has become the "go-to" publication to learn about early stage company valuations, given the dearth of alternative treatises. Since some of these newer and unique valuation methodologies were introduced in 2004, however, the techniques have been refined, improved, and challenged in practice.

To address these refinements and improvements, this book, *Valuing Early Stage and Venture-Backed Companies*, provides a detailed, hands-on guide to value early stage companies, along with broad fundamental data on the venture capital industry. It provides detailed analyses of unique early stage company valuation approaches along with examples of generally accepted allocation models that address complex capital structures so common to early stage companies.

Some of the techniques discussed include:

- Back-solving valuation
- The modified cost approach
- The option-pricing model (OPM)
- The probability-weighted expected returns model (PWERM)
- Asian puts
- New data on discounts for lack of marketability

At times irreverent, the book mixes real-life experience with deep technical expertise to produce a user-friendly guide to valuing early stage companies, which many practitioners consider the hardest to value. The AICPA practice aid is currently being updated as well, so there will be more than one alternative for students and practitioners wanting to learn more about valuing early stage companies.

NEIL J. BEATON, CPA/ABV, CFA, ASA
Grant Thornton LLP

Acknowledgments

I want to acknowledge a number of folks who contributed to and reviewed the drafts of this book: Ted Wang of Fenwick & West, and Bob Duffy, Dave Dufendach, Scott Beauchene, Andy Ross, Michele Kleyn, Candice Bassell, Stillian Ghaidarov, John Sawyer, and Jason Andrews of Grant Thornton LLP.

I also want to thank Char Connolly for her editing and the folks at John Wiley & Sons for their Job-like patience as I missed deadline after deadline.

Acknowledgments

I want to acknowledge a number of folks who contributed to and reviewed the drafts of this book: Ted Wang, Dr. Fenwick E. West, and Bob Ulrey, Dave Pahneback, Scott Beaubiere, Andy Ross, Michele Klevp, Candace Bassel, William Childers, John Sawyer, and Daryl Andrews of Grant Thornton LLP.

I also want to thank Laurie Connolly for her editing and the folks at John Wiley & Sons Periodical Publishing patience as I missed deadline after deadline.

About the Author

Neil J. Beaton is the National Partner in Charge of Grant Thornton LLP's valuation services. He has more than 25 years of experience analyzing both closely held and publicly traded companies but has focused much of his unbounded energy on valuing early stage, venture-backed companies. Beaton has appeared as an expert witness in numerous courts around the world, lectures at local universities, is an instructor for the AICPA's business valuation courses, and speaks nationally on business valuation topics, with a special emphasis on early stage and high-technology companies. Beaton served on the original AICPA "cheap stock" task force responsible for publishing the practice aid *Valuation of Privately-Held-Company Equity Securities Issued as Compensation.* He is currently co-chair of the AICPA's "cheap stock" task force that is in the midst of updating the original practice aid. He has served on the AICPA's National Accreditation Commission and the FASB's Valuation Resource Group. Beaton has a BA in economics from Stanford University and an MBA in finance from National University. In addition to his formal education, Neil is a Certified Public Accountant Accredited in Business Valuation, a Chartered Financial Analyst, and an Accredited Senior Appraiser in business valuation from the American Society of Appraisers.

Valuing Early Stage and Venture-Backed Companies

CHAPTER 1

Laying the Foundation

This book doesn't profess to have all the answers, but it will provide solutions for, and alternatives to, many valuation issues faced by early stage, venture-backed companies. Furthermore, this book is not a treatise on proper accounting treatment; other books are available that cover that topic, and it should be said that there is little consensus among accounting firms as to how a particular issue should be treated. However, this book does provide an experiential and practical guide to valuing early stage, venture-backed companies. It incorporates what I've learned during more than 15 years of focused start-up work along with the collective wisdom of the many practitioners whom I've had the joy and honor to work with over the years.

A UNIQUE LANDSCAPE

To really understand the context in which early stage companies are valued, a thorough background of the different economic and socioeconomic environments in which such companies exist is needed. In addition, a working understanding of the venture capital industry is helpful, given that venture capital is the engine that powers these companies to success (success is the goal, even though it's not always achieved). The following paragraphs and sections lay the basic groundwork for the unique aspects of valuing early stage companies.

Readers who were performing valuations during the dot-com boom of the late 1990s are familiar with the crazy valuations that were prevalent at the time for early stage companies. Early stage companies, those with

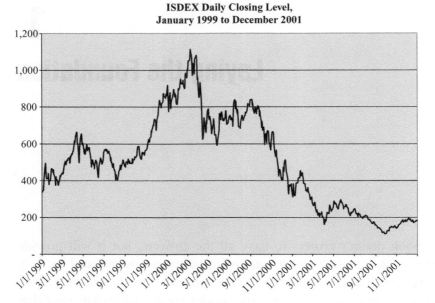

**ISDEX Daily Closing Level,
January 1999 to December 2001**

EXHIBIT 1.1   Internet Stock Index, January 1999 to December 2001

little or no revenue or income, were commanding huge valuations, some-times eclipsing the market values of many well-established "old economy" companies. I look back fondly at that time, recalling how any valuation, no matter how ridiculous, seemed to be accepted—and even revered—by the investing public. Valuation professionals could make no mistake, and "experts" such as Henry Blodgett and Mary Meeker achieved iconic status. But reality finally set in, and the bubble burst with a bang during March and April 2000, as shown in the Internet Stock Index (ISDEX) chart in Exhibit 1.1.

A telling story is that the ISDEX is no longer published as of this writing. Even more telling, however, is that during the two-plus years from December 1999 through February 2002, more than 800 Internet-related companies went out of business, according to Webmergers. The carnage is shown in Exhibit 1.2, which displays an expected inverse of the ISDEX chart and also supports the adage that what goes up must come down.

Ironically, as all of these start-ups began to start down, a new start-up entered the scene in April 2000, *Fucked Company*, which chronicled the plight of failing Internet companies with humor and irreverence. Styled after *Fast Company*, a magazine for start-up technology companies that is still in circulation, *Fucked Company* followed the same path of the very companies

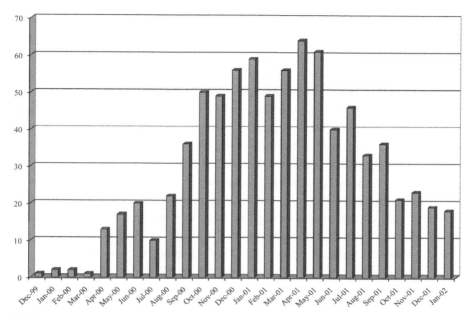

EXHIBIT 1.2 Internet Shutdowns and Bankruptcies by Month, December 1999–February 2002

Source: Data from Webmergers, Inc.

it ridiculed, ultimately being sold to TechCrunch in April 2007, seven years after its illustrious start.

At this point, readers may be asking, what does all of this have to do with valuing early stage companies? The fact is that there are no hard-and-fast rules in valuing early stage companies. Although it can be said that valuing closely held companies is more art than science, that statement is even more applicable to early stage companies. A fledgling start-up has too many unknowns, ranging from an inexperienced management team to an iffy customer base to an uncertain market for initial public offerings. When a prominent venture capital expert was asked what figures into his valuations, he answered, "Three guys, a garage, a product, or a beta site."

We've often heard that hindsight is 20/20. Looking back at the dot-com bubble, I wonder how in the world things got so crazy! I believe the answer lies at the core of valuation theory, and specifically in one aspect of that theory—uncertainty. Fundamentally, valuation professionals need only three basic items to value any asset (and I'm not referring to "three guys, a garage, and a product"): (1) an income stream, (2) a discount rate, and (3) a growth rate. A seasoned valuation professional can consider those three things and then value the asset. However, when one or more of those items is unknown or uncertain, the underlying valuation becomes murky. For early stage companies, at least two of the three necessary inputs are subject to substantial uncertainty.

First, the income stream is sometimes little more than an "Excel exercise" based on a spreadsheet model that is typically built on numerous, untested assumptions. Second, the growth of the income stream is a pure SWAG (i.e., scientific wild-ass guess). The importance of the discount rate under these circumstances diminishes—without a relevant and reliable income stream or growth rate, what is there to discount?

So what was driving such high valuations during the late 1990s? Clearly the Internet played a big role, but that is only on the supply side. On the demand side, capital was flowing like beer at a frat party. This is shown in Exhibit 1.3, which demonstrates the amount of capital committed to venture funds at various times from 1980 through the second quarter of 2009 (annualized). Notice what happened in 1999 and 2000 and even during the residual period in 2001. The stock market frenzy during that time was a capital and business siren beckoning both investor and entrepreneur to drink the Kool-Aid of high valuations. Initial public offerings (IPOs) hit feverish highs, mirroring the amounts of capital companies were able to raise. After a sobering up in 2002, the trend resumed as venture capital commitments began a slow and cautious return through 2007, when the

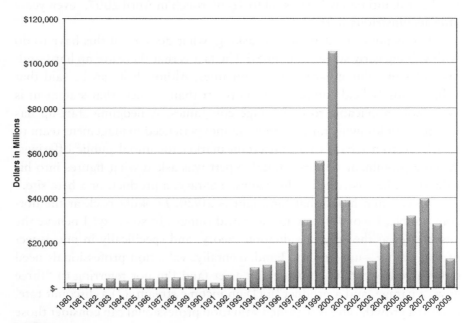

EXHIBIT 1.3 Venture Capital Commitments by Year

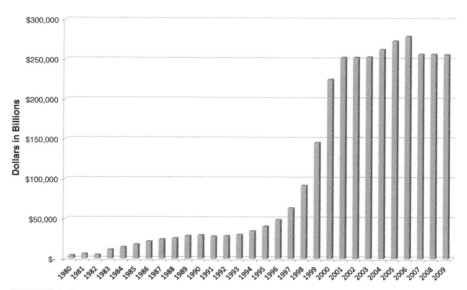

EXHIBIT 1.4   Venture Capital under Management

current economic crisis put the brakes on committed capital. The second quarter of 2009 showed the lowest number of funds raising capital since 1996 and the lowest raising of capital since 2003.

However, even though capital commitments have slowed, the amount of venture capital sitting on the sidelines waiting for an opportunity to play is staggering, as shown in Exhibit 1.4. More than $250 billion (with a "b") of capital has been looking for a home since 2001. Interestingly, given the amount of capital raised per year shown in the foregoing chart, it appears that during the past nine years what has been raised has essentially been invested. The lesson to be learned here is that there is plenty of money available to invest but a perceived lack of investment opportunities. What does this say about current valuations?

The ultimate goal of any venture capital (VC) fund is to create value for its investors. One thing VC funds focus on to accomplish this goal is liquidity for their investments, which take the form of either mergers/acquisitions or IPOs. As shown in Exhibit 1.5, both the number of IPOs and the amount of capital raised by these IPO companies peaked between the last quarter of 1999 and the first quarter of 2000. Many paper millions were made by thousands of new investors, and some were even lucky enough to sell off before the big crash and convert at least some of their paper profits into real dollars.

The majority, however, were not as fortunate. VC investing plummeted, and IPOs went on a two-year chill. But as with most things in business,

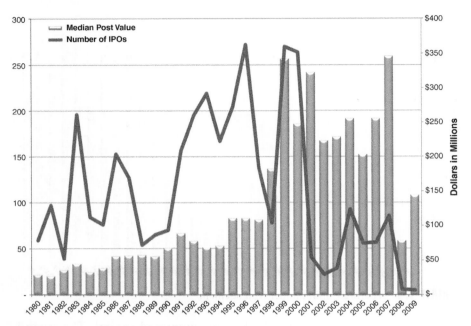

EXHIBIT 1.5 Venture-Backed IPOs

the cycle returned; new investment increased, and IPOs began to emerge from the dot-com debacle through 2007. What goes around comes around, though, and a new nadir was reached in 2008, when only five IPOs went out. During the second quarter of 2009, as many new venture-backed IPOs went out as in all of 2008, but currently, it is not clear whether the IPO window will be open again, as it was in 1999 and 2000. I'd say that will be based on the converse of what goes up must come down (i.e., what comes down must go up).

Granted, tremendous business potential was created by the Internet, but no one really knew just how *much* potential there was. This uncertainty was the primary driver behind the run-up in valuations; investors were afraid that they would miss out if they didn't invest. Going back to our three valuation ingredients, cash flows were projected to increase at a phenomenal pace (remember "get big fast"?), while discount rates continued to be drawn from the general marketplace for the most part. Since most of these companies didn't have positive earnings before interest, taxes, depreciation, and amortization (EBITDA, a common measure of available cash flow), let alone earnings, revenue multiples replaced price-to-earnings (P/E) multiples. The moderation in multiples that one would expect from moving up in the income chain (net income to revenue), however, did not occur. Instead, new terms were invented to "fit" these absurd valuations.

A walk down memory lane brings to mind such valuation metrics as:

- Price to employees
- Price to page views
- Price to click-throughs
- Price to downloads
- Price to personal digital assistants
- Price to property, plant, and equipment (PPE)
- Price to doors passed
- Price to next year's revenue

You will notice a prevalent lack of financial metrics for obvious reasons. But Internet companies weren't the only ones looking for valuation validation in the marketplace. Infrastructure players, such as competitive local exchange carriers and cable companies, were being valued based on price to property, plant, and equipment or price to subscribers. Although nonfinancial metrics weren't new in the late 1990s, they were the *only* metrics on many occasions.

Performing a valuation engagement for an early stage company requires an approach that is different from a valuation engagement for a typical revenue and income-generating entity. The absence of financial metrics from which to derive value, coupled with intense uncertainty, mandates a different analytical skill set. Such assignments force the valuation professional to delve deeper into the qualitative aspects of the company, its management team, and its market prospects more than is typical in a "traditional" valuation engagement. These roles are discussed in more detail in the following sections.

Early stage company valuations are usually performed for the issuance of common stock options, but they can be done for other purposes as well. I am often asked to value an early stage company for investment purposes, but since most early stage companies already have a modicum of external investment, I tend to suggest a more advisory role than a formal valuation. In real life, the valuation of an early stage company is a result of a mutually accepted valuation between the company and its financial backer or backers. The valuation incorporates the entrepreneur's determination of the acceptable amount of ownership that may be given in return for the investor's capital or expertise as well as the investor's assessment of the risks and rewards of the investment. As such, understanding the valuation process both from the investor's perspective *and* the company's perspective is critical. The stage of development is also important and follows a pretty consistent path for most early stage companies.

Valuation methodologies differ by the stage of investment and the availability of quantitative and qualitative data. However, the basic components of early stage company valuations are universal and somewhat simple and should be understood before a potential investor takes on such an engagement. The following sections discuss how investors consider, construct, and justify valuations of early stage companies and offer perspective on the dynamic role of valuation throughout a company's life cycle. However, before I discuss the nitty-gritty of valuation, an overview of the venture capital industry—the primary source of funds for early stage companies—is helpful.

AN OVERVIEW OF THE VENTURE CAPITAL INDUSTRY

Venture capital is money provided to young, rapidly growing companies that have the potential for significant growth in the markets they serve. Venture capital is an important source of funding for start-up companies because many such companies do not have access to traditional sources of capital for their growth needs. Venture capital investing has grown from the small investment pools typical of the 1960s and the early 1970s to a mainstream asset class that is a viable and significant part of the institutional and corporate investment portfolio. As shown in Exhibit 1.3, total venture capital commitments (i.e., promises to provide money to the fund at some future point) and fund size were relatively stable from 1978 through 1994, before a sharp increase occurred in both categories from 1998 through 2000 with the advent of Internet-based companies like eBay and Amazon.com. Commitments dropped precipitously in 2001 and 2002 before edging up annually through 2007 and then dropping again in 2008 and 2009.

Investment Focus

Venture capitalists may be generalist or specialist investors depending on their investment strategy. Generalists invest in various industry sectors, various geographic locations, or various stages of a company's life. Alternatively, specialists focus on one or two industry sectors or seek to invest in only a localized geographic area or in a particular stage in a company's life cycle. As of 2007, there were approximately 740 venture capital firms

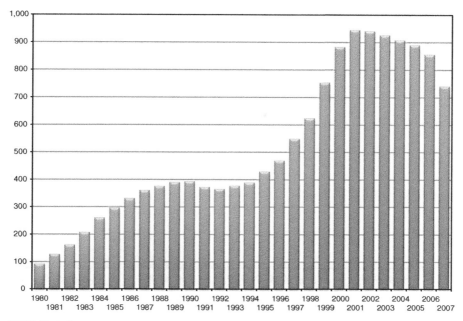

EXHIBIT 1.6 Existing Firms by Fund Vintage Year

representing 1,550 separate venture funds, more than eight times the number existing in 1980. Employment-wise, the industry had approximately 8,900 professionals managing more than $255 billion in venture capital spread over various "stages" of investment. Through 2007, more than 600 venture firms had exited the industry, about 200 of this total having exited since 2001, as shown in Exhibit 1.6.

Venture firms often invest in start-up companies, but they also invest in companies at various stages of the business life cycle. "Seed" investing (investment made before there is a real product or company organized), "early stage" investing (investment in companies in their first or second stages of development), and "expansion stage" investing (financing a company to allow growth beyond a critical mass to become more successful) are common categories of venture investing. There are other "stage" breakdowns disseminated by various organizations, including the National Venture Capital Association (NVCA) and the American Institute of Certified Public Accountants (AICPA), but they are generally in agreement.

Exhibit 1.7 shows the amount of investment by stage from 1990 through the first quarter of 2009 (annualized). The significant amount of expansion—second- and third-stage funding during 1999 and 2000—resulted from a change in investor attitudes toward risk. Before the

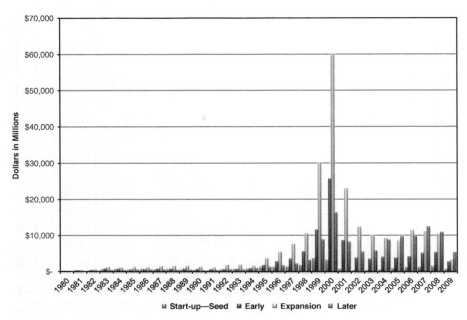

EXHIBIT 1.7 Venture Capital Investments by Stage

Internet bubble burst, investors were willing to "bet" significant sums on potentially huge market opportunities. However, the realities of the current market environment have slaked that thirst; overall investment fell considerably during 2003; it inched up from 2005 through 2007 but fell again in 2008 and 2009 as the prevailing economic sentiment took its toll.

While high-technology investment makes up most of the venture investing in the United States and the venture industry receives a lot of attention for its high-technology investments, venture capitalists also invest in enterprises such as construction companies, manufacturers of industrial products, and providers of business services. Venture firms come in various sizes, from small, seed specialist firms with only a few million dollars under management to firms that have more than a billion dollars in capital invested around the world. What all these types of venture investing have in common is that venture capitalists are not passive investors; they have an active and vested interest in guiding, leading, and growing the companies they have invested in. They seek to add value through their experience in investing in tens and hundreds of companies.

As Exhibit 1.8 shows, over the long term, venture capitalists have been quite successful in generating substantial net internal rates of return for their investors for the periods measured. However, timing is everything.

EXHIBIT 1.8   Performance of Venture Capital Funds, 2008

Fund Type	1-Yr	3-Yr	5-Yr	10-Yr	20-Yr
Early/Seed VC	25.6%	6.8%	3.1%	34.5%	20.8%
Balanced VC	35.4%	14.6%	10.1%	14.9%	14.2%
Later Stage VC	38.2%	11.6%	9.0%	8.6%	13.9%
All Venture	31.3%	10.7%	6.9%	17.9%	16.4%

The 1999 and 2000 vintage funds actually had negative returns at the one- and three-year measurement points. Fortunately, most funds were able to continue holding their investments until they could sell for nominal returns of at least three percent.

Length of Investment

Venture capitalists generally like to exit their investments in three to seven years. However, an early stage investment may take seven to twelve years to mature, whereas a later stage investment may take only a few years; consequently, the appetite for the investment life cycle must be congruent with the limited partnerships' appetite for liquidity. Most venture investments are illiquid until distributions have been made by the general partner. As Exhibit 1.9 shows, venture investments, in terms of both number of deals and amount of investment, have slowed considerably from their peak in 2000 and are currently on par with pre-1997 levels.

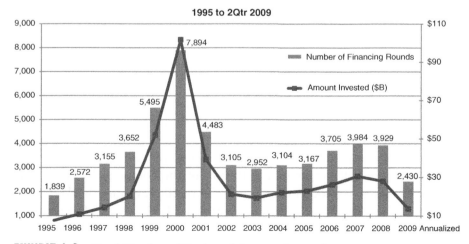

EXHIBIT 1.9   Total Number of Deals and Amount Invested

Capital Calls

Making investments in portfolio companies requires the venture firm to start "calling" its limited partner commitments. The firm will collect or "call" the needed investment capital from the limited partners in a series of tranches commonly known as "capital calls." These capital calls from the limited partners to the venture fund are sometimes called "takedowns" or "paid-in capital." Although some firms call this capital down in equal installments, many venture firms now try to match their funding cycles with their capital needs and therefore call their capital on an as-needed basis.

Illiquidity

Limited partners make investments in venture funds with the understanding that the investment will most likely be for the long term. It may take several years before the first investments start to return proceeds; in many cases, the invested capital may be tied up in an investment for seven to ten years. Limited partners generally factor this illiquidity into their investment decisions. Exhibit 1.10 demonstrates the volatility related to limited partner distributions. As shown, limited partners experienced substantial investment returns in 1999 and 2000 before the bottom fell out in 2001 and 2002. Distributions climbed back up in 2004 and 2005 before flattening again in 2006 and remaining there through 2007. Overlaying this chart with Exhibit 1.3 reveals that distributions lag commitments on a year-to-year comparison, but what isn't known is how long those particular limited partners (LPs) had to wait for their specific distribution. Many funds have multiple distributions, given that underlying portfolio companies are either sold or have an IPO.

Exits

As noted previously, VCs seek to exit their investments within three to seven years of the initial investment. While an IPO may be the most glamorous and heralded type of exit for the venture capitalist and owners of the company, the most successful exits of venture investments have occurred through a merger or acquisition of the company by either the original founders or another company. Prior to 2001, venture-backed IPOs dominated the markets, as shown by Exhibit 1.11. However, after the tech wreck in 2000, venture-backed IPOs have struggled because investors have been wary about wading back into the "tech IPO" pool.

12

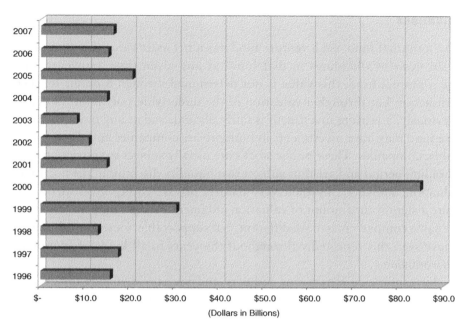

EXHIBIT 1.10   VC Limited Partner Distributions

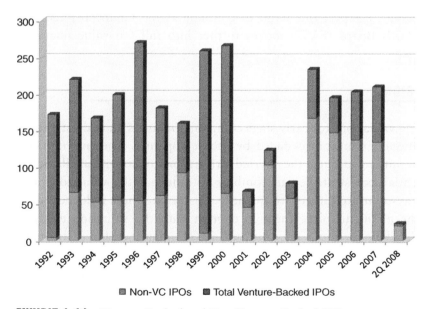

■ Non-VC IPOs   ■ Total Venture-Backed IPOs

EXHIBIT 1.11   Venture-Backed and Non-Venture-Backed IPOs

Valuations

Like a mutual fund, each venture fund has a net asset value (i.e., the value of an investor's holdings in that fund) at any given time. However, unlike a mutual fund, this value is not determined through a public market transaction but through a valuation of the underlying portfolio. As noted previously, a venture investment is fairly illiquid, and at any point the venture fund may have investments in both private companies and the stock of public companies. These public stocks are usually subject to restrictions for a holding period and are thus subject to a liquidity discount in the portfolio valuation. However, by their very nature, private equity investments require a significant amount of valuation judgment. Accordingly, investors in the same company may have different, but supportable, views on valuation. I have seen this repeatedly throughout the years in all kinds of economic environments.

In response to a maturing industry and investor demands for greater transparency and valuation consistency, the Private Equity Industry Guidelines Group (PEIGG) was formed in 2003 to deal with the issue of valuation guidelines. The first version of the guidelines was issued in 2003, and they have been continually updated and refined since then. The latest guidelines can be found at www.peigg.org. With the advent of fair value requirements for portfolio investments, venture funds have been slowly but surely engaging in more stringent valuation exercises for their portfolio companies. I expect this trend to continue as the Financial Accounting Standards Board (FASB) moves further into full fair-value financial statements.

CONCLUSION

Performing valuations for early stage companies requires an understanding of the unique circumstances faced by such companies. The environment in which funding occurs, the myriad drivers of investment availability, and potential exit strategies all combine to influence the valuation process in ways that are difficult to quantify. Discerning these influences and having the ability to place them in context with the valuation engagement will allow for more relevant and useful valuations for early stage companies.

Exhibit 1.12 (shown on the following pages) summarizes many of the differences in perspective between a VC and a common stock investor.

EXHIBIT 1.12 Summary of Differences in Perspectives of Venture Capitalists and Common Stock Investors

	Venture Capitalists	"The Rest of Us"
Investment Focus	VCs are usually well diversified with respect to companies in the sector(s) they target. They usually have superior access to industry and company information as compared with common shareholders.	Common stock investors typically have most of their investment concentrated in the company with little or no diversification. In addition, common stock investors typically have limited access to information about other private companies or alternative investments.
Length of Investment	As discussed previously, VCs have the ability and expectation to wait three to seven years for their returns, and in some cases as long as ten years.	Common stockholders typically do not have the wealth or risk tolerance to be comfortable waiting this long for their return. They usually value long-term investments significantly lower than would a VC.
Capital Calls	VCs are not concerned about where the money for future investments is coming from (i.e., once they close fund raising for their next fund). Often, there is a potential "agency affect"; it is not their money and therefore they will manage it appropriately.	Common stock investors put in their own money (albeit in the form of sweat equity or foregone salary). This creates the antithesis of the "agency affect." Common stock investors often can't protect their investment by buying into the next rounds, and so forth.
Illiquidity	By their very nature, VCs are more comfortable with illiquidity than other types of investors, since their investment horizon is long. Moreover, they have access to emerging secondary markets for sales of limited partner units that are not available to common investors (or at least rarely). Finally, they have access to their other portfolio companies and peer portfolio companies for potential mergers and/or sales, neither of which are available to the typical common stock investor.	The common stock investor is less forgiving of illiquidity and has fewer (often no) options for mitigating illiquidity compared to the VCs. One could expect that a common stock investor would put a much higher discount on the same asset as compared with the VCs.

(Continued)

EXHIBIT 1.12 (Continued)

	Venture Capitalists	"The Rest of Us"
Exits	VCs have a priority position and can obtain a return *of* capital and maybe even a return *on* capital in a number of scenarios.	Common stock investors are generally at the low end of the capital structure and typically need a "home run" in order to see any return on, or of, their investment. While discounts may address this potential lack of timing, it is not clear whether current valuation techniques adequately reflect the perspective of the common stock investor.
Valuations	Because they are typically well diversified, VCs are more comfortable with a range of valuations. For example, if one of their portfolio companies fails, they have other companies that hopefully (and statistics back this) do quite well. VCs have been successful, as a whole, in creating superior returns for their limited partners.	Common stock investors are much more sensitive to valuations. Being well down in the capital structure, they need a "home run" to achieve a decent return; because they are un-diversified, this "home run" must be *their* company. Having no liquidity (as compared to at least some for the VC), they need a liquidity event to happen sooner rather than later. Given all these factors, it isn't surprising that a common stock investor might look at exactly the same set of financial statements and other information and end up putting a much lower value on the same security than the VC, let alone one that is by design inferior to the VC's (i.e., common vs. preferred).

CHAPTER 2

Understanding Early Stage Preferred Stock Rights

Most early stage companies raise external capital through the issuance of preferred stock. Institutional venture capitalists (VCs) and other early stage investors prefer the additional risk protection afforded by preferred stock. This "protection" can be divided between financial and managerial or control protections, all of which have a different impact on applicable discounts, which are discussed in Chapter 6. Make no mistake, though; this preferred stock is not the plain vanilla preferred stock your grandpa and grandma invested in as a safe investment alternative. Rather, preferred shares typically issued to VCs and other early stage investors are often extremely complex financial instruments with unusual and even exotic provisions. It is the interplay of these provisions that make this financial instrument so potent and pervasive among early stage investors.

As we review these provisions individually, it should be noted that their potency and relevance change over time as the underlying investee company progresses through its stages of development. Whereas a liquidation preference may be extremely relevant for a Series A round, it may be much less relevant for a Series E round, where the company is on the verge of a sale or going public. With that in mind, let's discuss these provisions and their potential impact on early stage company value.

Preferred stock gives its holders numerous rights and privileges that common stockholders do not enjoy. These rights and privileges explain some, if not most, of the fair market value differential between preferred stock and common stock. These provisions are used to provide investors with downside protection as well as some additional control over management and company activities. Moreover, investors use these provisions to align the incentives of the company's management team, which typically holds common stock, with the investor's investment objectives. Preferred stock is ultimately a vehicle with which companies attempt to satisfy investor demands in order to attract capital.

The core rights of preferred stock are typically set forth in a company's organizing documents. For Delaware corporations, the organizing document is known as a Certificate of Incorporation. These core rights are discussed in the following text and account for the most important differences between preferred and common stock. Other rights typically granted to holders of preferred stock are found not in the company's organizing document but rather in separate contracts (e.g., an Investor's Rights Agreement). These rights are discussed in a later section.

It goes without saying, but it is still important to note, that the rights and privileges of preferred stock exist only so long as preferred holders do not convert to common stock. As discussed subsequently, preferred stockholders can give up their preferred rights and convert to common stock, often at any time and at their discretion. The dynamics surrounding conversion underlie many of the important differences between preferred and common stock. Generally, preferred stockholders are unlikely to convert. Instead, they typically choose to hold onto their preferred stock and benefit from higher returns and control over the company. This "option" may be difficult to measure, but it clearly possesses value to the holder. The valuation techniques presented in this book attempt to capture this "option" value, but it is often elusive; it even differs among VCs, companies, industries, and economic cycles.

When a company does well and has an initial public offering (IPO) or successful sale, preferred stockholders are usually forced to give up their preferred rights and convert to common stock. It is rare that any preferred shareholders remain after a sale, and almost never after an IPO, but there are some instances when it does occur. Not that the preferred shareholders wouldn't have converted anyway to reap even higher returns, but practically, the new owners in a sale scenario generally want to strip away the power preferred stock bestows on its holders, and preferred investors desire the liquidity of publicly traded common stock or cash to basically illiquid preferred stock. The essential goal of preferred stock is to create an incentive structure so that common stockholders are rewarded with high returns as long as the preferred stockholders receive their superior returns first. It is a delicate interplay, but it is expected by most early stage companies looking for institutional venture capital investment.

STOCK RIGHTS

The company's organizing, or corporate, documents specify the core rights of preferred stock. Some rights are economic, designed to provide better returns for preferred stock as compared with those for common stock. Others are control rights that give preferred stockholders the ability to influence and even control the company in a manner that is disproportionate to their ownership percentages.

Economic Rights

The following are five of the more common economic rights found in preferred stock issued for venture capital investments in private companies:

1. Liquidation preferences
2. Preferred dividends
3. Redemption rights
4. Conversion rights
5. Antidilution rights

Generally, these economic rights relate to timing, preference, and amount of returns for preferred stock relative to common stock. Preferred stockholders with favorable terms can create opportunities for upside while securing downside protection and incentivizing management to perform well.

Liquidation Preferences   Liquidation preferences account for perhaps the most important differences between preferred and common stock because they govern the distribution of asset value in liquidation. Liquidation can be positive or negative. A positive liquidity event primarily relates to a merger, acquisition, or IPO, whereas a negative liquidity event would be the cessation of operations with an orderly or forced liquidation. This is significant because sales transactions (either a merger or an outright acquisition) represent the most common exit for venture-backed private companies. In every year since 2001, more than 80 percent of venture-backed liquidity events were merger or acquisition deals, while fewer than 20 percent were IPOs.[1] Exhibit 2.1 provides updated statistics on exit probabilities through the second quarter of 2009.

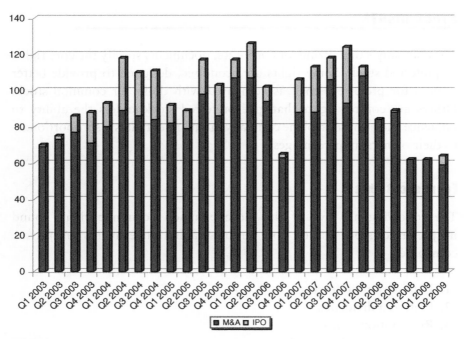

EXHIBIT 2.1 Venture-Backed Liquidity Events by Quarter, 2003–2009

In distributing assets or proceeds from sale, the liquidation preference gives priority to preferred stockholders, ensuring that they are paid
some amount (called the preference amount) before any portion can be distributed to the common stockholders. Typically, preferred stock receives
its original investment (or even some multiple of its investment) and potentially a preferred return before the common stock receives any distribution. Establishing this order of payout affords preferred stockholders some
downside protection in the event the company fails to perform. Moreover,
it ensures that management, which typically pays a nominal amount for its
common stock, is not rewarded for achieving a poor outcome. In certain
cases the preference amount can be more than the initial purchase price.
This is usually expressed as a multiple (e.g., 2x) of the original price. Occasionally cumulative dividends are added to the initial preference amount,
thereby raising the bar for management by some amount every year. Although cumulative dividends, or any dividends for that matter, are hardly
ever paid out, a cumulative dividend provides another layer of "protection"
or return potential if the company is ultimately successful.

In addition to the preference amount, preferred holders may also receive
preferred returns through what is called participation. Under participation,
after the preference amount is paid to the preferred shareholders from the

liquidation proceeds, preferred shareholders may participate further in the distribution of the remaining proceeds. There are two types of participation: (1) partially participating (or capped participating) preferred and (2) fully participating (or uncapped) preferred. There is also nonparticipating preferred, in which the preferred stockholders receive no additional proceeds other than their initial preference amount.

"Nonparticipating preferred" means that preferred stock does not participate with the common stock in the distribution of remaining assets after receipt of the initial preference amount. This is the least desirable type of participation for the preferred stockholder, but statistics indicate that about a third of all preferred stock financings do not have a participating feature. Yet what VC or investor would agree to these less favorable terms if they didn't have to? The answer, of course, is that it depends. It usually depends on who has the strongest negotiating position, the VC or the company. And in the realm of early stage investing, VCs usually prevail, as indicated by a study done by Dow Jones that shows 62.3 percent of all financings for participants responding to their survey issued participating preferred.[2] Remember the "golden rule": He who has the gold makes the rule. This "rule" is validated constantly in the early stage realm. That is not to say an early stage company won't have the stronger negotiating position; I have been involved with many such companies. During the later stages of the Internet craze, it happened more often than it has recently, but it still does occur consistently. The "strength" argument is borne out by statistics in that same study that indicate participating preferred was issued in 88.2 percent of all "flat" rounds and 75.0 percent of all "down" rounds. A "flat" round occurs when a subsequent financing is completed at the same valuation as the prior round. A "down" round occurs when a subsequent financing is completed at a lower valuation than the prior round.

VCs may also take nonparticipating positions in the early financing rounds because they are thinking about their exits and additional financing rounds involving other investors. If they ratchet up the participation rights too early in the process, they may set off a participation arms race that must be untangled or restructured before they achieve liquidity. I should also point out that even within financing events, a lead VC may receive a participating position, but the follow-on VCs may not.

Nonetheless, participation provisions don't necessarily cap the return a preferred holder can obtain. First, as noted previously, the initial preference amount can be a multiple of the original issue price. Second, the holder of preferred stock can convert to common stock if doing so produces a superior economic result. If the value of the common stock exceeds the preference amount, preferred would convert to common and all stockholders would share equally on a per-share basis. Additionally, cumulative dividends, discussed previously, may augment the preferred stockholder's return even without any participation.

"Partially participating preferred" means that preferred stock does participate, but with the amount of participation capped at some multiple (usually between 2x and 4x) of the preferred stock purchase price. This cap has the effect of placing a ceiling on the amount a preferred stockholder can receive through participation. More important, it has the effect of aligning the incentives of preferred and common stockholders. Recall that preferred stockholders have the option of either retaining their preference and participation or converting to common. With a cap on participation, common stockholders know that some valuation threshold exists above which preferred stockholders will find it more beneficial to convert to common. The 2008 Dow Jones Venture Capital Deal Terms Report indicated that, of their respondents, 80.0 percent had capped participation of 1x compared to 76.9 percent in the 2007 study. Capped participation of 2x was present in 14.5 percent of all financings with 3x and above accounting for the remaining 5.5 percent in 2008. Comparable statistics were 16.7 percent for 2x and 6.4 percent for 3x and above in 2007.

Once the preferred converts, all of the preferences disappear, and the common shareholders share the entire proceeds on a pro rata basis (also known as sharing from first dollar). With this knowledge, common stockholders are incentivized to attain a target valuation above this threshold in order to induce conversion. The cap on participation thus aligns incentives because it gives common stockholders the possibility of sharing from first dollar, while providing preferred stockholders with a minimum return of investment on exits at moderate prices.

"Fully participating preferred" means that preferred stock participates in the distribution of remaining proceeds on a pro rata basis with the common stock, with no ceiling on the participation amount. Because there is no ceiling, holding onto preference and participation until the latest moment is always more attractive than early conversion. The consequence is that preferred stockholders rarely voluntarily convert into common stock in connection with an exit. Moreover, unlike the benefit of capped participation, founders and employees do not have the added incentive of working toward a target valuation that would induce conversion. Common stockholders often object to participation rights because, regardless of the value of the company at exit, preferred holders are always able to "double dip" by getting their preference as well as a pro rata amount after they have received their investment back. This gets back to the negotiating position previously mentioned. Nevertheless, the "golden rule" again applies in this instance, and the fully participating preferred is a very common formulation. As a matter of fact, the "golden rule" is pervasive in the early stage financing world.

Preferred Dividends Preferred stock often possesses dividend rights that create additional differentiation from common stock. There are two types of dividend rights, but only one is normally relevant in the venture-backed company context. Noncumulative dividend rights, which merely provide priority to preferred stockholders before distribution to common stockholders, are meaningless; in practice, venture-backed companies do not pay dividends to common stockholders. Such rights often state that dividends will be distributed "when, as, and if declared." They continue to exist more as a block on any common dividends than as something intended to produce future cash flows to the preferred shareholders.

In contrast, cumulative dividend rights are important because they can translate into increased returns for preferred stockholders. Cumulative dividends accrue and must be paid before any liquidation, sale of the enterprise, or other liquidity event (typically excluding an IPO). In the most common formulation, accumulated dividends are added to the liquidation preference of the preferred shares, giving them an increased share of the proceeds in the event of a sale. Occasionally, the provision will allow the accumulated dividend to factor into the rate at which the preferred stock converts into common stock, resulting in a greater number of common shares being issued than would otherwise be available. This can have a huge impact in the case of a company exit because it can increase the number of shares of common stock that the owners of the preferred stock hold, thereby increasing their pro rata entitlement to proceeds. In either form, cumulative dividends are another protective device that adds value to preferred stock.

Redemption Rights Redemption is the repurchase of stock by the company. Preferred stock often has a mandatory redemption right, which allows preferred holders to require the company to repurchase their stock. The price can be either fixed, such as the original purchase price, or one that increases based on a formula, such as the original purchase price plus a redemption premium (typically an accumulated dividend or a price to be determined, such as the then-current fair market value). Technically, this right allows preferred stockholders to exit the company and redeem their investment (and receive some return) if the company does not achieve a milestone or reach a liquidity event within a certain investment horizon. In practice, however, investors cannot force a true redemption if the company has insufficient funds, which one would expect to be the case in a poorly performing company.

In other words, redemption is typically exercised only in the event the company cannot actually redeem the shares. Thus, mandatory redemption is more of a tool with which preferred stockholders require the company to explore liquidity alternatives, such as forcing a sale. Many redemption rights have a "hell or high water" provision forcing the company to make all possible efforts to sell itself to effectuate a redemption. The overall effect is to give the preferred investors an opportunity to realize some return on their investment if the company does not perform well, irrespective of the returns from such a transaction to the common stock—another potential rearing of the "golden rule" head.

Redemption rights are particularly important when viewed together with the preferred stock liquidation preference. If a company has a value below or not materially above its liquidation preference, common stockholders acting in a self-interested manner would be inclined to take risks that could jeopardize the company's current value but could potentially lead to a bigger reward. In such a case, preferred stockholders might opt to redeem their shares, force a low-dollar sale, and take a small return rather than go along with a high-risk bet.

Conversion Rights Preferred stockholders typically may convert to common stock at their discretion. This is called optional conversion because preferred stockholders have the option of converting when such conversion would produce superior economic results. Conversion rights typically include a provision for automatic conversion at certain events, such as an IPO or upon a vote of a majority of the preferred stock. The reason for the mandatory conversions are (1) to enable the company to convert preferred stockholders to common for events such as an IPO, in which case conversion will be practically required; and (2) to enable a forced conversion in the event it is required in circumstances such as a "down round" financing. Usually preferred stock converts into common on a one-to-one ratio, but the conversion ratio may be more favorable to preferred stockholders after certain dilutive events, as discussed in the following subsection.

Antidilution Rights   Antidilution rights prevent or reduce dilution of preferred stock in the event of subsequent "down rounds" of financing. A "down round" occurs when subsequent financing is made at valuations below prior-round valuations. Antidilution rights can be divided into two categories—full-ratchet and weighted average. Full-ratchet rights provide the strongest protection in the event of a down round. In the full-ratchet category, the original conversion price of the preferred stock adjusts to the new issuance price regardless of the dilutive effect of the new issuance. For example, if the preferred stockholders purchased shares at $10 and the company has a subsequent round of financing at $5 per share, the conversion price of the outstanding preferred shares will be adjusted to $5, doubling the amount of common shares to be received at conversion.

Weighted average antidilution is less protective because the adjustment in conversion price is tempered by a weighted formula that takes into account the magnitude of the dilution. This method factors in the sale price, the number of shares outstanding, and the number of shares sold better reflecting how cheap the new stock is and how large the new issuance is relative to the capital basis of the company. The formula works as follows:

$$\text{Issuance price before down round} * \frac{A + B}{A + C}$$

where
- A = outstanding fully diluted common shares
- B = number of shares that would have been issued at the old price * actual price
- C = number of shares actually issued * actual price

There are two types of weighted average antidilution—broad-based and narrow-based. Broad-based protection includes outstanding preferred stock and options in the calculation, whereas narrow-based protection excludes outstanding preferred stock and options from the calculation. Broad-based protection is favored by common stockholders because it causes less adjustment to the conversion price in the event of a dilutive financing. Conversely, narrow-based protection is favored by preferred stockholders because it increases the adjustment to the conversion price. The 2008 Dow Jones Venture Capital Deal Terms Report indicated that approximately 60 percent of respondents reported weighted-average antidilution provisions and approximately 15 percent reporting full-ratchet; about a quarter of respondents reported no antidilution provisions.

Typically, certain equity securities are carved out from antidilution such that no adjustment to the conversion price occurs. A typical carve-out is exemplified by employee stock options. Other typical carve-outs consist of securities issued to other "partners," such as equipment lessors, lenders, and strategic partners. These types of stock issuances are not formal equity financings; therefore, revaluing the preferred stock would be inappropriate on the basis of such a securities issuance.

Control Rights

In addition to rights that offer economic advantages, preferred stockholders have rights that provide elements of control over the company. While preferred stock typically votes on an "as if converted" basis with common stock, there are circumstances in which preferred stock has special voting rights. With these rights, preferred stockholders may exercise influence over company decisions in a manner that is disproportionate to their ownership percentages. The effect of these control rights is to gain influence over matters that could be relevant to the return on investment. Control rights would seem to be more relevant in the earlier stages of a company's development when there is greater uncertainty, but surprisingly, control rights are often tighter in later stage deals when success becomes more likely since investors want to assure their investment objectives continue to be met. The main levers of control are board representation, veto rights, or "voting by class" rights whereby certain corporate actions require the approval of preferred stockholders, but usually not common shareholders.

Board Representation Preferred holders usually require and are granted the right to elect a certain number of directors to the board. Board representation provides preferred stockholders with the ability to secure at least a minimum level of board influence at all times. It is not uncommon for preferred holders to have the ability to elect half of the directors, even if they own only a minority position in the company. Another conventional formulation involves allocating a board member for the preferred stockholders, a board member for the common stockholders, and a third member elected by both. The third (or other odd-numbered) seat is often the subject of a voting agreement requiring the mutual consent of preferred and common directors, thereby effectively increasing the control of the preferred stockholders. As the company goes through subsequent financings, the number of seats allocated to preferred stockholders usually increases, but the influence of each individual tranche (i.e., Series A, Series B, etc.) may wane.

Veto Rights   Apart from influence through board representation, preferred stockholders as a class may exercise control over their investments and the company by requiring approval in connection with various events. These veto rights give preferred stockholders the ability to block actions that might adversely affect them. The list of company actions subject to veto rights may include:

- Mergers or substantial sales of assets
- Adverse changes to the rights, preferences, and privileges of preferred stock
- New preferred stock issuances with rights equal to or superior to the preferred stock
- Redemption of stock
- Amendments to the Certificate of Incorporation or Bylaws
- Changes in the number of directors or reservation of seats for election by certain classes of stock
- Changes to the company's line of business
- Increasing the number of shares issuable under the company's stock option plan
- Hiring or firing of officers

Although preferred stockholders are able to exert control as they typically receive board representation for their investment, in theory board members are constrained by their fiduciary obligations to do what is in the best interest of the company. In contrast, "regular" stockholders generally have no such fiduciary obligations to other stockholders and thus can lawfully block company actions that might benefit the company as a whole but are contrary to their specific interests. Because of this, sophisticated investors will use their blocking rights to attempt to align the interests of the common and preferred stockholders. For example, a blocking right over a merger or other sale is used to motivate the common stockholders (i.e., management) to grow the value of the company to a point where the preferred stockholders have achieved a sufficient return. As the list of company actions subject to blocking rights expands, preferred stockholders can come to exert a substantial amount of control over a company's business.

CONTRACTUAL RIGHTS

In addition to the stock rights found in the company's charter documents, preferred stockholders may obtain other rights through separate agreements with the company and other stakeholders. These rights include:

1. Registration rights
2. Drag-along rights
3. Co-sale, or tag-along, agreements and rights of first refusal
4. Rights of first offer
5. Information rights

These rights can be quite valuable, thereby increasing the potential differential in value between preferred stock and common stock. For example, through certain contractual rights, preferred stockholders may obtain the ability to force an IPO, purchase founders' stock, secure a certain portion of future financings, or access the financial information. Pay-to-play provisions, which are usually found in a company's Certificate of Incorporation, can also become important and impact the value of a company's equity securities.

Registration Rights

Registration rights provide a path to liquidity by allowing preferred stockholders to force the company to register its stock with the Securities and Exchange Commission (SEC) for sale in public markets. There are several types of registration rights that can occur at different points in a company's development and under different circumstances.

While a company is private, demand rights allow preferred stockholders to force the company to register its preferred stock in an IPO, assuming they convert to common stock. In theory, this right forces management to take a company public even if it has plans to keep the company private and raise capital by different means. In practice, however, demand rights are rarely exercised; if the company is ready to go public, there is little need to demand registration, inasmuch as this would be an "aligned" goal of the investors and the company. Furthermore, the opportunity to affect an IPO is very market dependent. If the IPO market is closed—that is, the market environment has conditions that are not favorable to IPOs, resulting in little if any activity—an investor's demand that a company file for an IPO is a mere waste of professional and legal fees. Exhibit 2.2 provides a history of

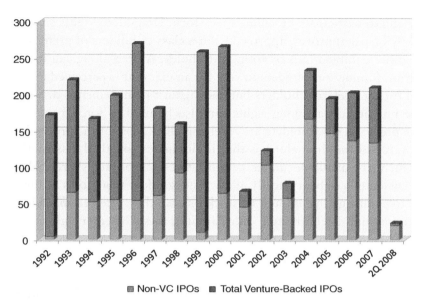

EXHIBIT 2.2 History of Venture-Backed IPOs

venture-backed IPOs. Notice that in 2001, 2002, and 2003, following the "tech wreck," very few companies were able to complete successful IPOs.

Another type of registration right, called an S-3 right, comes into play after a company has been public for 12 months. An S-3 right allows preferred stockholders to force an offering of their stock on a Form S-3, a simple and relatively inexpensive form of registration. S-3 rights are much less onerous for companies and provide preferred stockholders with an easily accessible avenue to liquidity if they so choose.

Often it is the company rather than the preferred stockholders that initiates an IPO. Under these circumstances, so-called piggyback rights allow preferred stockholders to join in the offering by requiring the company to include their converted stock. These rights are generally not available in an IPO because underwriters need to protect the marketability of the new stock and the success of the IPO. Similarly, outside of the IPO context, piggyback rights are often subject to cutbacks by the underwriter, because registering the additional stock may hamper the company's efforts to raise capital. Nevertheless, piggyback rights, when they are available, provide preferred stockholders with yet another additional avenue to liquidity.

Drag-Along Rights Drag-along rights are rights that force common stockholders (and often preferred stockholders) to vote for the sale of the company and to participate by selling their stock. Drag-along rights can be triggered by board approval, approval from a class of holders of preferred stock, or other combinations of voting thresholds. A drag-along can force a recalcitrant founder or founders to vote for an exit that is perceived to be beneficial for the preferred holders but goes against management's dreams of empire building. Drag-along rights can also be used to force a sale in which the preferred stockholders are receiving all or most of the proceeds. Another value of the drag-along is that it eliminates so-called dissenter's rights, which are available under certain states' corporate shareholder statutes. Dissenter's rights typically allow a stockholder who votes against a merger to challenge the amount of stock or cash they received in such a merger as "unfair." A contractual drag can limit these dissenter rights.

Co-Sale Agreement and Right of First Refusal   Preferred stockholders may also gain additional rights concerning the founders' stock. The right of first refusal allows preferred stockholders to cut in front of potential third-party buyers and buy the founder's stock at the same price that the third party was willing to pay. Similarly, co-sale or "tag-along" rights allow preferred stockholders to sell their stock side by side with the founder in a proposed sale to a third party. These rights are designed to prevent founders from cashing out early and make it both more difficult and less lucrative for a founder to do so. These rights further align the common and preferred stockholders by reducing the liquidity available to founders in one-off sales, thereby encouraging the founders to seek liquidity events for all stockholders, such as a change of control or an IPO.

Right of First Offer   In the context of new financings, the right of first offer gives preferred stockholders the right to invest a certain percentage of any future financing. Typically, preferred stockholders are allowed to invest enough to maintain their percentage ownership in the company. For this reason, the right of first offer is sometimes referred to as a "pro rata" right. Pro rata rights essentially provide an option to buy shares in the future at fair market value. This option has inherent value and is particularly valuable with successful early stage companies. If the company performs well, pro rata rights provide preferred stockholders with the opportunity to participate alongside other new investors. If some preferred stockholders with pro rata rights choose not to participate in the new financing, "over-allotment" rights allow the other preferred stockholders to buy the unpurchased shares. As with antidilution rights, employee stock or shares issued to service providers such as equipment lessors, lenders, and strategic partners are not subject to this right.

Information Rights   Preferred stockholders may also obtain information rights whereby the private company delivers certain financial information unavailable to common stockholders. Such information may include quarterly or monthly financial statements; annual audited statements; and annual budgets, forecasts, or operating plans. Some preferred stockholders may gain additional information rights, such as the right to make on-site inspections or observe board meetings. Typically, there is a threshold amount of shares required for a preferred stockholder to gain access to private company information. Information rights provide preferred stockholders with exceptional means to monitor their investments.

Pay-to-Play Provisions   As noted previously, pay-to-play provisions are usually contained in a company's charter documents, but are discussed here since such provisions can have a significant impact on the pricing of a company's securities. Pay-to-play provisions allow the latest-round preferred shareholders to require prior-round investors, usually in earlier preferred rounds, to participate in the current round of financing or suffer some economic consequence. A common "penalty" for *not* participating is a forced conversion to common of the prior holders' preferred shares. There are variations, of course, but the principle is to require economic participation to provide a greater cushion for future operations. Depending on whether the upstream preferred shareholders decide to "pay-to-play," the common shareholders could benefit or be irreparably harmed. For example, if the junior preferred shareholders decide not to "pay" and are forced to convert to common or take a lower preference payment, that value may accrue to the common stockholders. On the other hand, the decision of the junior preferred shareholders not to "pay" may signal the impending doom of the company, since these junior preferred shareholders may have decided it is better not to "throw good money after bad."

A spike in pay-to-play provisions occurred during the last quarter of 2008 and through the first half of 2009, when many investors assessed their exposure and desired some additional protection. However, a recent VC survey noted that these have become less frequent after the year-end spike when the market reversed its downward trend and more VC capital began to flow into follow-on deals. Pay-to-play provisions were reported in 37 percent of deals during 2004, but steadily decreased to 15.2 percent of all

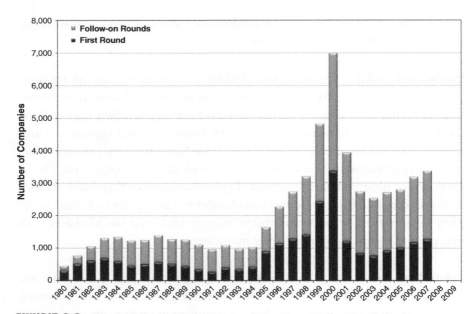

EXHIBIT 2.3 Venture Capital Investments—First versus Follow-on Rounds

reported deals in 2008, reflecting, in part, improving economic conditions during this time. It is my contention that the prevalence of pay-to-play provisions, after increasing throughout 2009, will level off in 2010 when many economists expect the economy to turn around. Exhibit 2.3 shows the long trend of first versus follow-on financings from 1980 through 2007 (the latest available data).

CONCLUSION

Preferred stock offers its holders valuable benefits such as enhanced returns, downside protection, and additional control over company decisions that affect their investments. Moreover, the rights and privileges of preferred stock serve the important purpose of aligning incentives of investors and management. Preferred stock rights are not perfunctory; rather, they provide substantive and meaningful advantages over common stock. In the valuation of early stage companies, it is important to understand the interplay of preferred stock rights vis-à-vis common stock as well as these preferred rights' relevance at different stages of a company's development.

Determining the value impact of each of these provisions is difficult, given that the measurement of these provisions is a moving target depending on a company's stage of development, its negotiating strength, its investors, the current economic environment, and other external factors. Experience is the best teacher when it comes to this very judgmental area of early stage company valuation.

Determine the value impact of each of these provisions is difficult, given that the instrument of these provisions is a moving target depending on a company's stage of development, its negotiating strength, its investors, and the current economic environment, and other external factors. Experience is the best teacher when it comes to the very judgmental area of early stage company valuation.

CHAPTER 3

Enterprise Valuation Approaches

In general, the subject of enterprise value approaches has been covered extensively in a number of excellent texts authored by Shannon Pratt, Jay Fishman, Robert Reilly, Jim Hitchner, Gary Trugman, and others, including the original Audit and Accounting Practice Aid Series, published by the American Institute of Certified Public Accountants (AICPA), known as *Valuation of Privately-Held-Company Equity Securities Issued as Compensation*. Regardless of the purpose of the valuation or the stage of development of the subject company, there are still only three valuation approaches to consider—income, market, and cost. It is not my intent to rehash what has been written elsewhere about these approaches. Enterprise valuation is simply the input (e.g., in the option-pricing model) or the result (e.g., in the probability-weighted expected returns method or advance option-pricing models) of equity allocation methods described in Chapters 4 and 5 of this book. Where the ultimate goal is to estimate the value of a particular class of equity (typically common stock), enterprise valuation methods represent the first step toward that objective.

The characteristics of early stage companies and the valuation approaches that are typically applicable at each of those stages are described farther along in this chapter. In addition, some concepts related to the cost approach that may apply in the valuation of early stage companies are introduced. This chapter describes some special considerations in connection with the application of the three approaches in the valuation of early stage companies.

RELEVANCY OF TRADITIONAL VALUATION APPROACHES

First, it is necessary to define the three valuation approaches as they relate to early stage companies. In preference to a typical definition from an accounting or valuation standard, the following definitions are meant to capture the essence of how I apply them to early stage companies:

- *Income approach*. This approach is a way of calculating the returns on a current investment based on the present value of forecasted cash flows or a future liquidity event. More often than not, investors in early stage companies and even the companies themselves don't receive or generate interim cash flows that are distributable. Therefore, under the income approach, a liquidity event may be the only opportunity for some security holders to receive a return of or on their investment. The option-pricing method can be considered an income approach.
- *Market approach*. This approach involves using substitute equity values as a proxy for the value of the subject security. More often than not, when I receive a call from an early stage company that needs a valuation performed, the company has recently had an infusion of capital through outside investment. The term sheet—that is, the document that sets forth the terms by which external investors are willing to invest—lays out the pre- and post-money values implied by the investment. Whether it is right or wrong (there are many reasons why a term sheet may not be an accurate presentation of a company's value), a term sheet provides a piece of dry land in a sea of uncertain company values for the analyst to begin his or her work toward determining a specific value input. The probability-weighted expected returns method can be considered a market approach.
- *Cost approach*. This approach is a measure of historical cost or the original amount invested that is used as a proxy for value when no value above that cost is perceived to have been created. Least often used, the cost approach is applicable only to a very narrow set of circumstances. By their nature, most start-ups are short on capital and long on ideas. Thus, if value exists, it is usually intangible and typically not captured by dollars invested. However, there are times (described more fully in a following section of this chapter) in which the company is in a very early stage of development or is about to go through a restart when the cost approach is the only reasonable valuation approach to use.

When selecting the right approach to apply to the valuation of an early stage company, I take a pragmatic perspective. Traditional valuation metrics are difficult to apply to companies with no revenue and no immediate prospect for positive cash flow. Rather than work from a predefined concept of which approach is preferable, the valuation of stock for equity compensation purposes requires us to analyze the facts and circumstances and select the most appropriate approach or approaches. At its basic practical level, the valuation of an early stage company necessarily depends on the data available, and this fact may drive whether "a valuation of stock based on a reasonable application of a reasonable valuation method is treated as reflecting the fair market value of the stock."[1]

A "Non-Traditional" Enterprise Valuation Method

How does one go about valuing a company with no revenue and, in many cases, no immediate near-term prospects for positive cash flow? Some specific methods are discussed in the following sections, but for very early stage companies without any prior investment, one way to estimate value is to look at the relationship of investment, give-up, and company stage of development. Assuming the company has "legs" (i.e., has demonstrated or perceived potential beyond a mere idea), the appraiser can look to information similar to that provided in Chapter 1 derived from data provided by the National Venture Capital Association (NVCA). Of the three valuation approaches cited above, this method can be considered a hybrid of the market and cost approaches. It is important to place a company's "value" in context when traditional valuation metrics, such as cash flow, are nonexistent. Relying on data provided by the NVCA helps place very early stage valuations in context since the data is fairly consistent over time and over stages.

An example may be helpful. Suppose an appraiser is provided with a business plan of a seed stage company that is looking for $750,000 to prove the technical feasibility of its software product, a new spreadsheet that will focus on the emerging DNA sequencing market. The business plan calls for an additional $1.5 million in capital needed in 12 months for the build-out of a sales force and management team. So far, the company has been funded by friends and family to the tune of $250,000. The founder and majority shareholder believes the company is worth $5 million but has no empirical support for that value. How does one go about determining the value of such a company?

The question is a little unfair in that very limited information has been provided to make an assessment. However, this is often the case with very early stage companies. So given this information, what would I do? First, since it's a seed stage company, I'd look to the median values for seed stage companies and see that they typically come in at around $2.5 million,

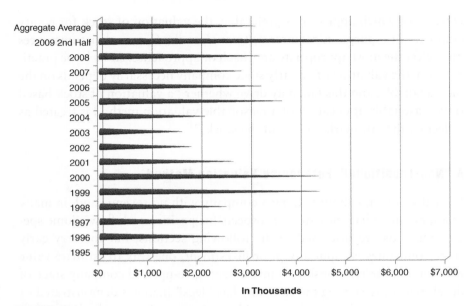

EXHIBIT 3.1 Average Start-up/Seed Investment by Year

according to VentureOne data. In addition, as shown in Exhibit 3.1, the average "start-up/seed" investment was around $3.1 million.

Okay, that's one data point. I know that the average give-up for seed stage companies is 27 percent (more data on this appears later in this chapter). So if the company gets $750,000, its implied value is $2.8 million ($750,000 ÷ 27% = $2.8 million). That's a second data point. However, I also "know" that the company will need an additional $1.5 million in a year to meet its expansion plans and achieve its revenue targets. I "know" still further that the average length of time to obtain follow-up financing is between 15 and 20 months. Finally, I "know" the step-up in value between the seed and the first round is about 20 times. Given all this, I estimate a value between $1.25 million and $1.75 million, pre-money.

Of course, it helps to have seen hundreds of business plans and early stage companies to get a sense of where this particular company and management team fits in. Additionally, such a valuation cannot be done in a vacuum; the qualitative risk factors discussed later in this chapter must be considered along with the quantitative data utilized. It is also instructive to look at overall valuations compared to the amount of external funds a company has raised during its build-out. Exhibit 3.2 illustrates this relationship from 1992 through 2005. Although the following data is only through 2005, the relationship between amounts raised and liquidity have been fairly steady except for the Internet bubble of 1999–2000.

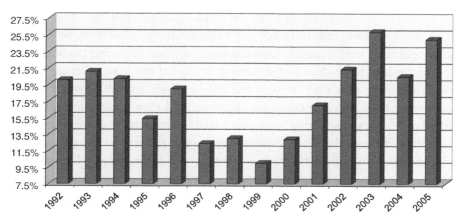

EXHIBIT 3.2 Amount Raised to Liquidity as a Percentage of Liquidity Value (1992–2005)

Exhibit 3.2 reveals a familiar pattern. From 1992 through 1996 (before the Internet bubble began to inflate), the amount of capital a company needed to raise was approximately 20 percent of its ultimate liquidity value. Then, during the bubble, from 1997 through the first quarter of 2000, the "liquidity percentage" dropped to around 10 percent. Following the bubble's burst, however, the pendulum swung back, with the liquidity percentage peaking at 25 percent and then settling back to above 20 percent ever since. Industry participants believe these ratios are here to stay; most VCs do not expect the excesses of the Internet bubble to return in any of our lifetimes. There may be occasional companies that bring us back to the crazy excesses of the bubble (e.g., some of the social networking sites), but overall, the bubble-bursting hangover continues to exert some restraint on overall valuations. This relationship becomes a solid benchmark from which to assess the reasonableness of a particular company's value at a particular point in time.

As mentioned briefly, since the tech wreck in 2000, one form of financing has become more prevalent—restarts. Restarts typically occur when a company has encountered unforeseen hurdles that have momentarily de-railed the implementation of its business plan. The underlying fundamentals of the business remain, but the timing to market may have been off. I have seen this occur again in the current equity market after the 2008 market liquidity crisis. Under these circumstances, historical results lose their relevance, making way for a new set of "milestones" with which future results will be compared. Restart financings are also known as "flat rounds" or "down rounds," in which valuation is reduced.

A down round can result from premature capital shortages that result from overspending, failure to achieve value-creating milestones, or suboptimal operating performance. Overpricing of a prior financing (as occurred during the Internet bubble) or softening of capital markets (as is currently occurring) may also play a role in a flat or down round. Down rounds are undesirable; they are cause for dilution, and they undermine investor confidence. They also bring unwanted write-downs to venture investors' portfolios, if they take them. Nonetheless, some restarts have had successful outcomes after going through a down round. Interestingly, I have been involved in lawsuits involving restarts in which the prior equity holders were "eliminated" in a down round only to see "their" company become successful under the tutelage of—and with additional capital from—follow-on investors.

Although the valuation of an early stage company at discrete points in time is subject to a certain range of interpretation, most seasoned venture investors and appraisers will value a company within a fairly tight range of each other if they have exhausted all quantitative and qualitative data available. It is difficult to say what causes this, but the empirical data clearly shows a fairly tight range of values for companies in a particular stage of investment. In the end, the minutiae of valuation will matter very little to a company with a solid product and market potential. Valuation can make a good investment more attractive, but it will not salvage a poor one. This is a big-picture concept that is often missed by management when assessing the motivational nature of incentive equity compensation plans. A company will usually receive several financings, and therefore valuations, before a liquidity event is accomplished. Building value is the shared objective of entrepreneur and investor. A mutual understanding between investor and entrepreneur of the risks and rewards driving a valuation is crucial to the ultimate success of the company and its investors.

COST APPROACH

The AICPA Practice Aid noted previously describes this approach as the "asset-based approach" and considers it the weakest from a conceptual standpoint. In fact, historical costs are not likely to be a reliable indicator of value where value is defined as the present value of future cash flows.

However, is it possible for a cost approach to satisfy the reasonable application of a reasonable valuation method standard even when it does not capture potential future value? I answer with a resounding "yes!" When the other approaches are based on information that is too speculative or difficult to support, investors would consider the amount invested to date in their estimate of the value of the stock as a relevant factor. Furthermore, as mentioned previously, investors in these types of companies are not typically relying on sophisticated discounted cash flow models or even market-comparable transactions to price their investment. Instead, a decision is being made about how much additional funding is necessary to take the company through the next operational milestone and how much ownership investors should receive for funding the next step. This type of real option analysis is described in Chapter 7.

Therefore, when I'm thinking about the cost approach, I'm often taking it from the perspective of the investment that has been made. For example, I often get involved with companies that have not incurred meaningful costs that could be measured using the absolute cost or modified option cost methods (described in more detail in the following sections). However, they may have received a significant first round of financing. In this situation, one could argue that the investors are paying an amount that recognizes the creation of value to date, but that should not necessarily imply that anyone believes the entire company could currently sell for the pro rata value based on the last round price. Here are some examples to clarify this point.

Example 1: An Initial Investment

Investors make an initial investment in preferred stock that represents one-third of the post-money capitalization of the enterprise. This Series A preferred stock has a liquidation preference of $1.00. After the Series A investors receive their liquidation preference in a liquidity transaction, common stock receives proceeds until the point at which it is financially advantageous for the Series A to convert to common. This structure is sometimes referred to as "common friendly," because the Series A does not participate with the common stock.

Equity	Shares	Issue Price	Total Investment
Preferred A	3,333	$1.00	$ 3,333
Common	6,667	NA	NA
Total	10,000		
Implied value based on last round			
	Shares	Price	Value
	10,000	$1.00	$10,000

These values will show up on term sheets for the financing round as pre-money and post-money values. In this case, the pre-money value is $6,667 and the post-money value is $10,000. Based on the post-money value, can the company be sold on the next day for $10,000? Absolutely not, nor is the intent of the venture capitalist investing in the company to liquidate the company the next day. Calculations of implied value based on the last round without considering the vectoring factors described previously and the rights and preferences of each equity class can result in implied values that are not reflective of the intent of the investors or the reality of the investment at that time. Although a lot of consideration is given to the issue price, it is primarily a method for determining the relative future equity ownership of the company. The associated rights and preferences tell the rest of the story as to whether the round is "down" or "up" in pricing. Without consideration of the rights and preferences, the implied value based on this scenario is $10,000. On the other hand, the $3,333 in the company's coffers could be the entire value of the company at that time. The answer likely lies somewhere in between the investment amount of $3,333 and the fully diluted amount of $10,000. In Chapter 4, we will calculate an implied "solve-for" value of the equity based on rights and preferences.

Example 2: More Shares, Same Investment

If instead the Series A preferred were priced at $0.50 per share but the same investment in terms of dollars were made, the relationship changes. More give-up of ownership of the company by the common shareholders represents a negative result to those common shareholders and results in less implied value. I've taken the same investment of $3,333 and the same common shares, but I've changed the price of the preferred to $0.50 and increased the shares accordingly.

Equity	Shares	Issue Price	Total Investment
Preferred A	6,666	$0.50	$3,333
Common	6,667	NA	NA
Total	13,333		
Implied value based on last round			
	Shares	Price	Value
	13,333	$0.50	$6,667

This is a down round relative to the $1.00 price in Example 1 since the $0.50 issue price in Example 2 is lower than that of Example 1. The floor value of the enterprise is still the $3,333 invested, but the ceiling has declined from $10,000 to $6,667. The issue price of the preferred is only one factor. The rights and preferences also impact the value.

Example 3: Example 1 with Different Preferences

If only the rights and preferences are changed from Example 1, the term sheet value is unaffected. The following are some conditions that can enhance the value of the preferred relative to the common:

- Preferred A stock has 2x liquidation preference so that the common stock will not receive any proceeds unless a liquidity event occurs at a value higher than $6,667 as opposed to $3,333 in Example 1. The common stockholders do not participate before the 2x threshold has been reached.
- Preferred A stock participates with a cap at 2x in the proceeds alongside the common stock after receiving its liquidation preference. With these terms, it takes a higher value before the common stock receives the same return.
- Preferred A stock participates without a cap, which results in the absence of any rationale for the preferred stock to ever convert to common stock unless forced through automatic conversion in an initial public offering (IPO).

In each of these situations, the term sheet pre- and post-money values are the same as in Example 1, but the value of the common stock is considerably different under each example. These examples show why you cannot rely solely on term-sheet values to establish the enterprise value of the company without consideration of the rights and preferences of the preferred stock. The solve-for method incorporates the rights and preferences and is discussed in Chapter 4. However, in each of these examples, the investment in the company was $3,333. Investment cost can be a more reliable reference point than post-money value.

MARKET APPROACH

There are many publications, including the original AICPA Practice Aid, that address the application of the market approach. There are three primary uses for the market approach in the valuation of an early stage company that has a complex equity capital structure. The first methodology is the estimation of the equity value as the underlying asset value input using the option-pricing method. The second methodology is the estimation of the future value of the company upon an expected exit. Finally, the third methodology under the market approach is often captured in a solve-for calculation alluded to previously and is described more fully in Chapter 4.

The application of the market approach in the option-pricing method is similar to the valuation of any company using the market approach. If the company has progressed sufficiently to have positive cash flow, or perhaps just revenue, market multiples derived from transactions and publicly traded stock can be applied using traditional market approach methods. Often with early stage companies, market approach methodologies may be based on higher-level parameters than we would typically choose to apply in a rigorous valuation analysis. These metrics may include:

- Post-money values of companies at similar stages of development in the same industry
- Target IPO ranges—for example, looking at biotech IPOs for a client and finding that the range of IPO values is fairly consistent between companies and over different years
- Transactions in which only aggregate equity values are known and no price/revenue or price/cash flow multiples are available

Application of the market approach to the valuation of early stage companies is discussed in Chapter 5, in connection with the scenario-based approaches. In a scenario-based analysis, future exit values are estimated based on projected revenue and earnings applied to multiples from guideline company transactions of companies at a similar stage of development. For example, a company that completed a successful IPO after launching its major product release may give useful price multiples to apply to the subject company at a future IPO date exit scenario if the subject company has progressed to a similar development stage at the future IPO date.

This application of the market approach is supported by the Internal Revenue Service and AICPA guidance. Internal Revenue Code (IRC) Section 409A, which is related to valuation, notes that "One commentator requested that the factors to be considered in determining the fair market value of the stock should be modified to include consideration of any recent equity sales made by the corporation in arm's-length transactions. The final regulations adopt this suggestion." Whereas Revenue Ruling 59-60 requires consideration of transactions in the company's stock, the IRC 409A definition seems broader and appears to support the use of the solve-for analysis of a recent financing round to calculate the value of the stock based on other equity classes. This is an example of how IRS guidance may overlap with the financial reporting guidance from the AICPA Practice Aid.

INCOME APPROACH

Although the income approach may be the most theoretically correct and appropriate methodology for an early stage company with considerable growth projected, the assumptions underlying a revenue and expense forecast can be extremely challenging to document and support. The common view is that the only truth about projections for early stage companies is that they are certain to be incorrect the next day. However, no other approach allows potential investors to specifically model the rationale for an investment in the company, including needed expenditures and identification of future financing needs. A detailed discussion of the income approach lies outside the scope of this book and is sufficiently covered in other appraisal literature noted previously. However, a few considerations in the application of the income approach to early stage companies should be noted, as follows:

- Because the development of projections for an early stage company depends on contingent outcomes and milestones, the common "one-scenario" expected cash flow model is often inadequate. An illustration of a method to value the cash flows based on the contingent outcomes appears in Chapter 7.
  - Typical early stage discounted cash flow analyses deal with questions such as "Can the company meet revenue targets and control costs?"
  - In addition, early stage companies deal with questions such as "Can we build a successful product and commercialize it? If not, then what?" Many social networking sites can drive heavy traffic to their sites but have difficulty monetizing that traffic.
- The risk of failure for early stage companies is difficult to capture in the present value discount rate derived using traditional capital asset pricing models. As an alternative, these present value discount rates are often supported by venture capital returns. However, these VC returns primarily relate to portfolios of investments. Therefore the rates represent an average of hugely successful investments that pay back multiples of the investment value and investments that net no return.

- As such, a present value discount rate may not capture the risk of any one investment when applied to one expected cash flow scenario as well as multiple scenarios might. As a result, multiple scenarios should be considered even if more disciplined contingent outcome analysis is not conducted. The probability of failure is often assessed well in the scenario-based allocation methods, but not as well in the option-pricing method. As a result, an option-pricing method allocation of equity can overstate the value of the subject common stock relative to other approaches if it is not fully vetted with considered knowledge.
- The vast majority of forecasts prepared for early stage companies show interim losses for at least a few years. Biotechnology companies, in particular, project losses for 10 years or more until Food and Drug Administration approval is expected to be obtained. In my review of many valuation reports prepared by a vast array of professionals using a discounted cash flow model under the income approach, I have seen many, if not most, practitioners discount interim losses at the company's cost of capital, be it an equity rate or weighted average cost of capital. In doing so, the implication is that these interim losses are somehow less risky vis-à-vis positive interim earnings or cash flow. In my experience, however, most early stage forecasts are too optimistic, even in regard to interim losses. Consequently, rather than using the company's cost of capital, I suggest practitioners use a risk-free rate of return. The use of a risk-free rate of return coincides with the risk profile of estimated losses. In other words, since the company is forecasting losses, it is highly likely that those losses, and even greater ones, will occur. Applying a risk-free rate to such interim losses recognizes the reality and difficulty of early stage company forecasting.

"VECTORING" VALUATION APPROACH

Like any investment process, early stage investing is far from an exact science. Early stage companies may consist of little more than an entrepreneur with an idea. Valuations at this early or "seed stage" are generally driven by factors that, by their nature, are subjective. These include:

- Assessment of the management team
- Compelling nature of the value proposition
- Evaluation of intellectual property
- Expected time to market

- Expected path to profitability
- Estimated capital needs and burn rate
- Industry sector volatility
- Deal structure

In later investment rounds, intermediate milestones such as events demonstrating technical feasibility and product validation will factor strongly in valuation determinations. As a company matures to the revenue and profit stage, more quantifiable data is produced in the form of operating statistics and performance indicators. Actual results allow investors more accurately to model quarterly and annual revenue, earnings before interest, taxes, depreciation, and amortization (EBITDA), cash burn, pipeline close rates, backlog, bookings, and enterprise valuation.

When there are so many "moving parts," it is difficult to specify a single methodology or approach to valuation. To address this, I created what I refer to as a "vectoring" approach to valuation. A vectoring approach considers a variety of inputs, some quantitative and some qualitative. Vectoring relies on common sense and industry practice as opposed to formulaic models that can be very accurate mathematically but fall so far from the mark as to be laughable. So how does one "vector" value? The following paragraphs provide some guidelines, but the reader must also bring his or her experience to the table as there are no hard-and-fast rules in vectoring.

As would be expected, the development stage of a company will also determine its relative value. What is interesting, however, is that the stage of a company also dictates the amount of capital the company is likely to acquire. Exhibit 3.3 illustrates these two observations clearly. As shown, first-time investment typically represents a smaller portion of overall venture investment. From 1980 to 2009, first-time investment represented only 26.5 percent of total VC investment. The big-dollar investments were generally reserved for later stage investment as companies were culled because of their failure to perform.

Exhibit 3.3 oversimplifies the valuation process, but it does indicate the valuation trend line of typical investments as companies mature. As those of us in the valuation profession know intimately, risk varies inversely with the quality and quantity of data. The high degree of uncertainty inherent in seed and early stage investments translates into relatively low pre-money valuations. Failure rates of start-up companies are extraordinarily high, so investors must be compensated for placing their capital at such risk. Conversely, later stage and mezzanine investors have the benefit of more certain financial models that help to mitigate

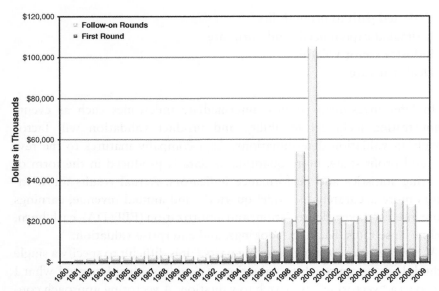

EXHIBIT 3.3   Venture Capital Investments—First versus Follow-on Rounds

risk. They "pay" for the reduced risk with higher pre-money valuations, lower step-ups, and lower overall returns (except for "mezzanine" financing, which usually occurs close to liquidity and realizes high returns), allowing for less upside. The last two phenomena are illustrated in Exhibits 3.4 and 3.5.

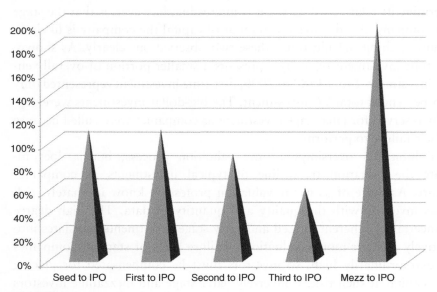

EXHIBIT 3.4   Returns by Stage to IPO

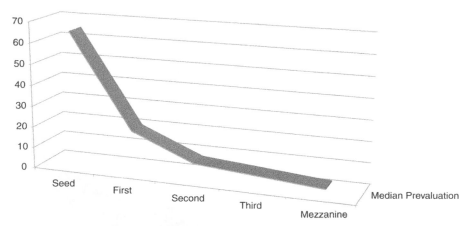

EXHIBIT 3.5   Median Value Step-ups by Round

Switching back to our "round" analysis, we now consider the amount of capital raised by each round. As shown in Exhibit 3.6, seed and first-round companies were generally at the bottom of the capital pile whereas second and later stage companies were at the top. The start-up/seed data for 2009 was skewed by an extremely large and unusual investment in a start-up/seed stage social networking company. Exhibit 3.7 shows the amount of capital raised by round from 1995 through the second half of 2009. It should also be noted that since the tech wreck, another form of financing

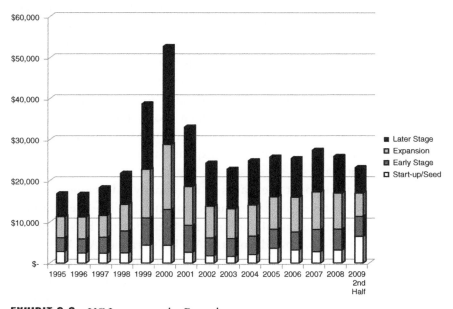

EXHIBIT 3.6   VC Investment by Round

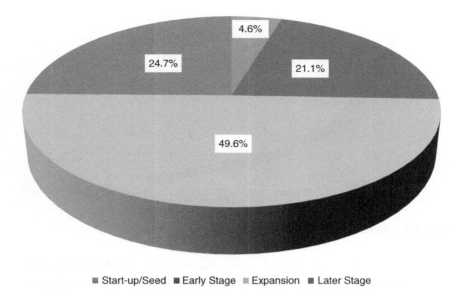

■ Start-up/Seed ■ Early Stage ■ Expansion ■ Later Stage

EXHIBIT 3.7 Percentage of Total Investment by Round 1995 through Q2 2009

(restart rounds) has begun to take on more prominence as companies that survived the wreck have been able to attempt a comeback of sorts.

The amount of capital raised is an integral input into the ultimate valuation model. Of note here, however, is the increasing amount of capital needed by round. Again, this is intuitive; one would expect companies in the second and later stages that are building out their production capacity and sales organizations to need a tremendous amount of capital. Another way of looking at this phenomenon is from the VC perspective. In Exhibit 3.8, seed rounds received very little venture capital, as most venture capital firms focus on first and second stage companies. But what is important here is the trend since 2000, which shows a steady increase in the percentage of venture capital into later stage companies. Of course, the brutal lessons learned in the tech wreck explain this movement to proven technologies or companies.

We've talked a lot about the stages of a company's development, but what are the typical stages for early stage companies? While there are no standards per se, consensus usually follows the breakdowns. This is shown in Exhibit 3.9, which is borrowed from the AICPA's Practice Aid *Valuation of Private Equity Securities Issued in Other Than a Business Combination.*

As set forth in the Practice Aid, there may be other stages an enterprise goes through that are not included in this table. Some product development cycles include extensive prototyping during development and

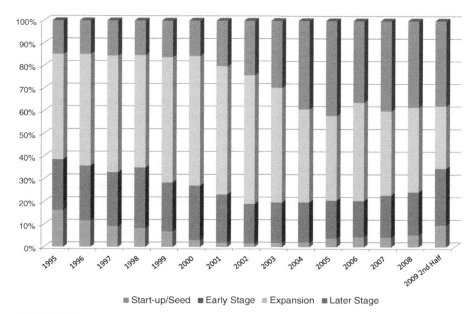

■ Start-up/Seed ■ Early Stage ▨ Expansion ■ Later Stage

EXHIBIT 3.8   Percent of VC Invested by Round, 1995 to 2009

may include many more stages than shown here. Moreover, not every enterprise necessarily goes through each stage.

The stage of development classifications used in the MoneyTree Report published by PricewaterhouseCoopers (PwC) are shown in Exhibit 3.10. These are the breakdowns used by PwC to report investments by stage in their quarterly and annual reports.

Yet another set of definitions for stages of venture-backed companies is provided in Exhibit 3.11 by the National Venture Capital Association (NVCA) with a little more breakdown than the PwC definitions just cited.

Valuations, of course, also vary by stage, as opposed to the "round" valuations that were explored previously. Based on data from VentureOne, Exhibit 3.12 shows the relative valuations of various venture-backed companies by stage of development.

As shown in Exhibit 3.12, continuous value increases are logged from the start-up through the shipping stage (*Note*: These "stages of development" are different from "financing rounds.") However, notice what happens in the "profitable" stage. The valuations are only slightly higher than in the "shipping" stage. Referring back to the discussion about value creation, this modest value increase at the "profitable" stage compared with the "shipping" stage can be traced to perception and decreased uncertainty.

EXHIBIT 3.9 Stages of Development in the AICPA Practice Aid

Stage	Description
1	Enterprise has no product revenue to date and limited expense history. It typically has an incomplete management team with an idea, a plan, and possibly some initial product development. Typically, seed capital or first-round financing is provided during this stage by friends and family, angels, or venture capital firms focusing on early stage enterprises, and the securities issued to those investors are occasionally in the form of common stock but more typically in the form of preferred stock.
2	Enterprise has no product revenue but substantive expense history, as product development is underway and business challenges are thought to be understood. Typically, a second or third round of financing occurs during this stage. Typical investors are venture capital firms, which may provide additional management or board of directors' expertise. The securities issued to those investors are most often in the form of preferred stock.
3	Enterprise has made significant progress in product development; key development milestones have been met (e.g., hiring of a management team); and development is near completion (e.g., alpha and beta testing), but generally there is no product revenue. Often, later rounds of financing occur during this stage. Typical investors are venture capital firms and strategic business partners. The securities issued to those investors are most often in the form of preferred stock.
4	Enterprise has met additional key development milestones (e.g., first customer orders, first revenue shipments) and has some product revenue but is still operating at a loss. Typically, mezzanine rounds of financing occur during this stage, and it is frequently in this stage that discussions start with investment banks for an IPO.
5	Enterprise has product revenue and has recently achieved breakthrough measures of financial success, such as operating profitability or breakeven or positive cash flows. A liquidity event of some sort, such as an IPO or a sale of the enterprise, might occur in this stage. The form of securities issued is typically all common stock, with any outstanding preferred converting to common upon an IPO (and perhaps upon other liquidity events).
6	Enterprise has an established financial history of profitable operations or generation of positive cash flows. An IPO might also occur during this stage.

EXHIBIT 3.10   Stages of Development Used by PricewaterhouseCoopers

- *Seed/start-up stage—the initial stage.* The company has a concept or product under development but is probably not fully operational. Usually it has been in existence for fewer than 18 months.
- *Early stage.* The company has a product or service in testing or pilot production. In some cases, the product may be commercially available but it may or may not be generating revenues. Usually the company has been in business for less than three years.
- *Expansion stage.* The product or service is in production and commercially available. The company demonstrates significant revenue growth but may not be showing a profit. Usually it has been in business for more than three years.
- *Later stage.* The product or service is widely available, and the company is generating ongoing revenue—probably positive cash flow. It is likely to be profitable, but not necessarily. It may include spin-offs of operating divisions of existing private companies and established private companies.

At the shipping stage, the ultimate profitability of the company is still unknown and valuations still contain a large dose of uncertainty. However, once profitability has been demonstrated and margins can be predicted with more accuracy, the uncertainty of future prospects is diminished, leading to more conservative valuations based on more realistic forecasts. Venture capitalists are no longer willing to pay for unknown future prospects at the profitable stage if those prospects are not expected to exceed their former expectations.

THE INCOME APPROACH AS AN OXYMORON

Venture capitalists review thousands of business plans each year. Data provided by Angelsoft, a Web-based service that assists investors obtain angel DNA venture funding, indicated that they reviewed more than 50,000 business plans from May 2008 through August 2009—almost 3,500 plans per month or more than 100 per day! And this is only *one* service for such investors. How many more are there? Most of these business plans are based on aggressive revenue and income growth assumptions and a rosy picture of the competitive landscape. Also, many claim to be predicated on "conservative assumptions," including minimal market penetration, product pricing, and gross margin. Regardless of how they are constructed, however, these plans are almost always overly optimistic in their assumptions.

I have had the opportunity to revisit the actual operating results of many early stage companies I valued in previous years; I have found that,

EXHIBIT 3.11 Stage Definitions Used by the NVCA

- **Early Stage Financing**
  - *Seed stage financing.* In this stage, a relatively small amount of capital is provided to an inventor or entrepreneur to prove a concept and to qualify for start-up capital. This may involve product development and market research as well as building a management team and developing a business plan, if the initial steps are successful. This is a pre-marketing stage.
  - *Start-up financing.* This stage provides financing to companies that are completing development and may include initial marketing efforts. A company may be in the process of organizing or may already have been in business for one year or less but it has not sold its products commercially. Usually such firms will have made market studies, assembled the key management team, developed a business plan, and are ready to conduct business.
  - *Other early stage financing.* Other early stage financing includes an increase in valuation, total size, and the per-share price for companies whose products are either in development or are commercially available. This involves the first round of financing following a company's start-up phase that involves an institutional venture capital fund. Seed and start-up financing typically involve angel investors more than institutional investors. The networking capabilities of the venture capitalist are used more in this stage than in more advanced stages.
- **Expansion Financing**
  - *Expansion stage financing.* This stage involves working capital for the initial expansion of a company that is producing and shipping and has growing accounts receivable and inventories. It may or may not be showing a profit. Some of the uses of capital may include further plant expansion, marketing, working capital, or development of an improved product. More institutional investors are more likely to be included along with initial investors from previous rounds. The venture capitalist's role in this stage evolves from a supportive role to a more strategic role.
- **Later Stage Financing**
  - *Later stage financing.* Capital in this stage is provided for companies that have reached a fairly stable growth rate—that is, they are not growing at the rates attained in the expansion stages. Again, these companies may or may not be profitable but they are more likely to be so than in previous stages of development. Other financial characteristics of these companies include positive cash flow.
  - *Bridge financing stage.* This stage is needed at times when a company plans to go public within six months to a year. Often bridge financing is structured so that it can be repaid from the proceeds of a public underwriting. It can also involve restructuring of major stockholder positions through secondary transactions. Restructuring is undertaken if there are early investors who want to reduce or liquidate their positions, or if management has changed and the stockholdings of the former management and their relatives and associates are being bought out to relieve a potential oversupply when the company goes public.
  - *Open market stage.* This stage involves acquiring securities of companies whose common shares trade publicly.

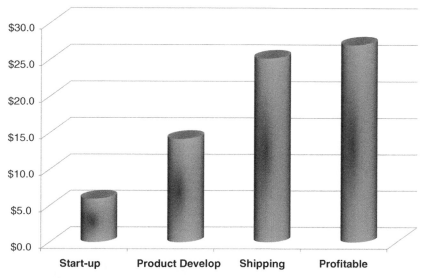

EXHIBIT 3.12   Median Pre-Money Valuation by Stage

except in rare occasions, their forecasts have proven wildly optimistic, if not in revenues, then at least on the expense side. A venture investor will usually "scrub the numbers," rationalize assumptions, and run sensitivities based on varying degrees of execution, competitive pricing pressure, seasonality, and the like. The resulting "adjusted" forecast may represent only a fraction of the original plan. As appraisers, it is often difficult for us to ascertain the validity of forecast assumptions, especially related to a unique technology or a novel drug. When we haven't done our own "scrubbing," we must deal with this uncertainty in the discount rate.

In spite of the difficulty of assessing the validity of forecasts, adjustments can be made based on management inquiry. For example, significantly greater capital requirements may be necessary. As appraisers, we must understand the short- and long-term capital requirements of the subject company. These capital requirements will provide the underpinning of the company's long-term financing strategy and answer the following questions: How much must be raised now? When will the company need to "go to the well" again? What significant milestones will be accomplished during that time? An understanding of the long-term financing strategy is crucial. As shown in Exhibit 3.13, the median time to a liquidity event has increased substantially since 1998 to a whopping 8.3 years. A slight decrease was experienced at the end of 2004 and into 2005 as the VC capital overhang (i.e., the amount of capital committed to venture funds) remained historically high and, coupled with an improving world economy,

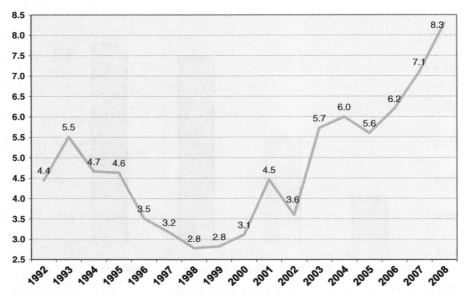

EXHIBIT 3.13 Median Time to Liquidity, in Years

had stimulated new investment. But that adjustment was short-lived in that the IPO window remained virtually shut to venture-backed companies, a situation persisting even at the time of this writing.

An important relationship to note when valuing early stage companies is the relationship between the post-money valuation as determined in a venture investment and the intrinsic market valuation of the enterprise that might be realized in a sale of the company at the time of that investment. The implied pre-money valuations of the seed and first-round investments usually exceed the intrinsic market valuations at the time of those investments based on sales of companies in these two stages. This is intuitive, given that the VCs are "betting" on the company ahead of the market. This early value premium results from the VCs' application of qualitative data derived from their collective experience or "gut" feelings about the prospects of the company. The venture investor is valuing the intangibles of the "idea" and human capital that the market may not "see" or be willing to pay for. As the company matures and moves into its second and third rounds of financing, pre-money valuations fall in relation to market value. Interim valuations are still generally below market value, but the gap closes considerably. This affords second-round and later investors a "risk premium" in valuation to compensate for the illiquid nature of private equity, even though much of the technological risk may have been sated.

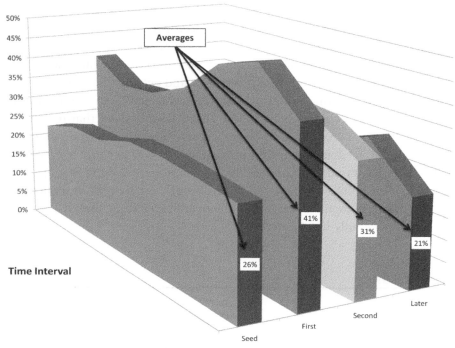

EXHIBIT 3.14   Equity "Give-Up" by Round

The foregoing risk and return perspective is primarily that of a VC. But what about the company's return perspective? What does a company have to give up in exchange for the funds a VC is willing to commit? Of course, the answer is *equity*—and many times with a big *E*! Ordinarily, each financing round is designed to provide capital for value-creating objectives. (This premise is violated only when capital is committed to "save" a company from an untimely failure until market or other conditions improve, but that is another story.) Assuming operating goals are accomplished and value is created, financing will continue at sequentially higher valuations commensurate with the progress made and risk mitigated.

Exhibit 3.14 shows what percentage of their companies entrepreneurs "give up" in exchange for each financing round. The patterns are interesting, however. Notice the amount of give-up at the first round. At 41 percent, entrepreneurs are giving up almost half of their companies, compared with an overall average of only 29 percent. Nonetheless, the relationships across rounds are fairly consistent, with the greatest give-up occurring at the first round, followed by the second round, and then the seed and later rounds. Although no definitive explanation for this phenomenon is given in the literature, I deduce that because the amount invested at the first stage is relatively greater than in typical seed rounds, and technological and market risk demons are still lurking around every corner, investors require a much greater amount of equity to compensate for the risk at that stage. At any rate, it is from these investment and give-up relationships that the appraiser can frame initial valuation conclusions. Statistics from the 2008 Dow Jones Venture Capital Deal Terms Report show that founders' ownership approximates 14.7 percent, on average, after a final round of financing. The median ownership percentage of 10.0 percent is even less and reveals the important fact that initial common ownership is subject to substantial dilution over the life of an early stage company. Consequently, it is important to factor dilution into the overall valuation analysis, a topic discussed more fully in Chapter 6.

CONCLUSION

This chapter covered a lot of data and ideas not normally addressed in traditional valuations. Valuing an early stage company without using solid value metrics is not a straightforward exercise by any means. Utilizing a forecast that was prepared at the hatching of an initial idea may be nothing more than an Excel exercise. Yet the early stage company appraiser doesn't have to go it alone. There is an abundance of data that can be used to frame a reasonable and relevant "story" in spite of a lack of hard financial data. It is the ability to take this seemingly disparate data and create a believable mosaic that sets the seasoned appraiser apart from the neophyte. Don't forget, however: There is no perfect method for valuing high-risk, long-term investments. First and foremost, investors look for a quality management team and then consider the prospects for the company. Only then can valuation be addressed.

CHAPTER 4

Application of the Option-Pricing Method in Allocating Enterprise Value

The option-pricing method is one of the most commonly used methods for allocating the aggregate enterprise value to the early stage company's various equity classes, including common stock. This method models the common and preferred stock as call options on the company's enterprise value. The claims on future distributable assets (i.e., enterprise value) depend on the rights and preferences of the company's preferred stock as opposed to its common stock. By modeling the common stock as a call option, the common stockholder is, in essence, given the right but not the obligation to buy the residual underlying enterprise value at a certain exercise price. Of course, in reality, the common shareholder really doesn't have the right to "buy" anything because the common stock is already owned. Nonetheless, modeling it as an option provides a similar economic construct as a true option since, if the company isn't successful, the "option" (i.e., the common stock) will expire worthless. The residual value available to the common stockholders is determined by an option analysis, described farther along in this chapter. Essentially, the residual value to the common stock is the remaining amount after the preferred stock liquidation preference and other participatory rights are measured.

As is the case with many early stage, venture-backed companies, the common stock options granted to employees are often considered "out of the money" at the valuation date, if not theoretically at least practically, given that such options are rarely exercised early. In other words, the common stock options have to be granted at the money under IRC 409A (henceforth, 409A), but I believe they have no practical value without a liquidity event; therefore, I consider them "out of the money" practically. This is because the immediate liquidation value of the typical venture-backed company is often below the liquidation preference carried by the preferred stock. However, the option-pricing method has as an underlying assumption that the company is a going concern and, as such, implies that there may be option value attributable to the common stock.

Even though common stock in a 409A analysis (in the old days such valuations were known as "cheap stock" valuations) is usually valued as of a specific date, the valuation and allocation methodology is typically forward looking. This assumption in and of itself precludes the use of the current method (discussed in Chapter 3). This concept is often ignored by, or lost on, many individuals involved in valuing early stage companies. Nonetheless, it is this particular attribute of the option-pricing model (that of attributing option value in all cases) that creates its schizophrenic behavior and requires the analyst to "get beyond the math" upon final inspection. More commentary on this appears later in the chapter. I should stress here that the option-pricing model in its most typical use is *not* a means of valuing the stock options to be issued to employees directly. Rather, it is a method for allocating the enterprise value of the company as an input to the subsequent valuation of the various classes of stock, including common stock. The option price of the common stock is determined separately, if the analysis is to be used under Statement of Financial Accounting Standards No. 123 (revised).

The option-pricing method lends itself to the valuation of common stock in early stage companies, since there are usually several years to a potential exit event and the timing, type (e.g., IPO, merger or acquisition, or staying private), and values of the future exit events are difficult, if not impossible, to accurately estimate. Actually, many practitioners claim it is these very attributes that also represent the Achilles' heel of the option-pricing method. Many practitioners believe that this method does not easily distinguish between the different outcomes that an IPO versus a sale of the company drives at a future exit event. When these future exit events can be reasonably estimated, a scenario-based allocation method—the probability-weighted expected return method (PWERM)—often provides a more relevant and reliable distribution of outcomes. However, when future events are highly uncertain—for example, at the seed stage of a company's development—the option-pricing method provides a means to estimate the value of common stock. Rather than assessing a relatively small number of discrete exit events that are typical when using the PWERM, the option-pricing method models a range of exit event scenarios *lognormally distributed* around the enterprise value. The enterprise (or equity) value at each of those future exit events modeled mathematically is then allocated to the preferred and common stock, based on the attributes of each class of security. Those discrete values are then probability-weighted and present valued back to the valuation date.

Typically, the common stock has positive value in scenarios where the future equity value of the company exceeds the preferred stock's liquidation preference and other economic rights that are superior to the common stock. As a consequence, the option-pricing method usually allocates some value to the common stock, even though the common stock, as represented as an option, may be "out of the money" if the company were to be immediately liquidated. Theoretically, the option-pricing method should be used only if the future potential exit event values can be reasonably estimated using a lognormal distribution. However, in the early stage realm of intense and unrelenting uncertainty, the practical identification of lognormally distributed returns is impossible. But to select only a few possible scenarios, even if they are appropriately distributed, leads to equally uncertain outcomes. That is why blind reliance on formulaic approaches is never appropriate.

Nonetheless, the option-pricing model is often utilized for making a reasonable estimate when the distribution curve is not known. When you stop and think about it, it is hard to fault a valuation professional for doing so. After valuing hundreds of early stage companies, I have concluded that any selected allocation model will never be precise. However, if you understand their shortcomings, these models will provide a reasonable and adequately reliable outcome. This reminds me of a statement made by my college English professor many years ago. He told our class that he was teaching us the rules of English not so that we would keep them, but rather that we'd know when to break them. He indicated it's acceptable to break the rules if you know them, but it's not okay if you don't. I believe the same philosophy holds in the valuation of early stage companies.

IMPORTANT ASSUMPTIONS UNDERLYING THE OPTION-PRICING MODEL

In general, option-pricing models fall into two categories: (1) the Black-Scholes-Merten (closed form) or (2) the binomial (open form) option-pricing models. For each of these models, there are six key assumptions: (1) underlying asset value, (2) exercise price, (3) term, (4) volatility, (5) risk-free rate, and (6) dividend yield. Option-pricing models are highly sensitive to each of these inputs; therefore, careful analysis and consideration must be used when selecting the inputs for the subject allocation.

Underlying Asset Value

The underlying asset value used in the option-pricing method is the company's enterprise value. However, determining an early stage company's enterprise value is one of the most difficult tasks valuation professionals face. In practice, venture capitalists and other early stage investors (myself included) guess wrong more than 75 percent of the time (the percentage of venture-backed companies that fail to achieve a liquidity event over time).[1] Nonetheless, as discussed in Chapter 3, various strategies are available for calculating this input.

We have noted that some valuation professionals use a total enterprise value, either including debt or excluding debt. Depending on whether debt is included or excluded, the first claim on value would switch from debt holders to preferred stockholders. The consideration of debt is typically not an issue for early stage companies, however, as it is next to impossible for early stage companies to obtain debt financing. There are a few banks focused on tech financing that will lend to early stage companies, but that debt is usually for hard asset financing secured by those assets, rather than true capital structure debt. However, depending on the unique circumstances of the company that is being valued, I would recommend starting with an enterprise value excluding debt (i.e., equity value), since it removes uncertainty related to estimating changes in the company's debt payoff schedule and the difficulty in estimating a levered volatility. Clearly, for companies lacking the characteristics of an early stage company listed in Chapter 3, the foregoing suggestions would not necessarily hold as traditional valuation techniques for handling levered capital structures exist and should be employed. But for a vast majority of early stage companies, the foregoing recommendations won't lead you too far astray.

Here is one additional thought on enterprise value. I have seen some practitioners take a discount for lack of marketability (see Chapter 6) *before* inputting the resulting enterprise value into the option-pricing model. I do not believe this is appropriate since at lower values the underlying asset value—in this case company value—won't cover the liquidation preferences or warrant or option values adequately. In general, the starting enterprise value marketability characteristics should match the exit event marketability. I have performed analyses indicating that taking a discount on enterprise value undervalues the residual common stock value by as much as 25 percent, depending on the size of the discount.

Exercise Price

In implementing the option-pricing method, multiple exercise prices that represent the enterprise value payouts at specified liquidity events are identified and calculated. The exercise prices at payout are calculated by modeling "breakpoints" that are unique to each company, based on the respective preferred and common stock claims on future distributable value. The liquidation preferences of the preferred stock are usually found in a company's Articles of Incorporation, but the term sheet and other corporate documents may also have to be reviewed for a thorough vetting of breakpoints. The breakpoints represent the future enterprise values at which there are changes in the distribution of proceeds among the various equity classes, including preferred stock, common stock, preferred and common stock warrants, and common stock options.

These changes are the result of the interplay between the various rights and preferences of each equity class—for example, there is typically a valuation breakpoint where the preferred stockholders have received their full liquidation preference and begin to participate with common stockholders if the preferred stock has a participating provision. There could be multiple breakpoints for a single issue of preferred stock or multiple breakpoints among various issues of preferred stock. The rights and preferences of each equity class are considered within this analysis, including liquidation preferences, participation rights, and conversion rights, among others. Let me stress here that this analysis creates a "hypothetical future" in which the common and preferred shareholders are nice to each other and split the proceeds of a hoped-for liquidity event. It doesn't always happen the way the model specifies, but the contractual provisions represent a reasonable base assumption.

In a basic option allocation model, the first breakpoint is generally the liquidation preference of the preferred stock. As such, upon a liquidity event, if the aggregate equity value of the company is at or below the liquidation preference of the preferred stock, then no value would be allocated to common stock because all the value, represented by the liquidated assets, would be allocated to the preferred stock. For the common stock to have value, the future enterprise value must be greater than the liquidation preference of the preferred stock. Under this assumption, we are able to calculate the estimated value of the common stock as represented by an option on the underlying enterprise value with an exercise price at the liquidation preference.

Often there are multiple exercise prices, depending on the conversion and participation rights of the preferred stock. For example, if the preferred stock is convertible, another exercise price would represent the equity value where the preferred stock would convert to common stock. If the future exit value is greater than that exercise price, the hypothetical proceeds would be distributed pro rata between the common stock and the preferred stock on an "as-converted" basis. Of course, breakpoints can get complicated when warrant and option breakpoints are included, especially if there have been a number of warrant or option grants at different strike prices that require different breakpoint analyses. Appendix A provides an example in which warrant and option breakpoints are analyzed. For simplicity, in this chapter, an example of the breakpoint calculation for one issue of preferred stock is provided in a following section.

Term

"Timing is everything." This is especially true for early stage companies facing an uncertain IPO or M&A market, usually the only exit events available for venture-backed companies. The term reflects the expected timing of a liquidity event. This assumption is often based on discussions with management and consideration of the following issues:

- *Company milestones.* The operational and funding milestones the company has to achieve prior to a liquidity event. This could include product development milestones, revenue run rates, cash flow benchmarks, and market acceptance metrics.
- *Investors' expectations and profile.* The investors' expectation of a likely return horizon for their investment. Most venture capital and private equity funds have five- to seven-year liquidity expectations (even though their agreements may indicate a term of up to 12 years).
- *Market and industry observations.* Trends within the marketplace and industry, including M&A and IPO activity, in addition to growth trends and the competitive landscape. As noted previously, the M&A and IPO markets virtually shut down in late 2008 with no indication of when they would open up again. Venture-backed companies experienced a similar closure of the M&A and IPO windows after the tech wreck in 2000.

Volatility

The volatility assumption relates to the expected volatility of the underlying asset over the selected term. Since the primary subject of this book is the valuation of early stage companies that are closely held with limited or no share activity, the volatility assumption is typically based on an analysis of guideline companies. Such an analysis should consider both historical volatility over the term horizon and implied volatility from public market participants. It is important to consider factors that may impact the development of a reasonable and supportable expected volatility estimate. The following items should be considered in the volatility selection:

- *Public company considerations.* If a market approach was used to determine the company's enterprise value (admittedly rare with early stage companies), such companies should be consistent with the guideline public companies used within that method. If the market approach is not used, public companies can still be identified within the subject company's industry; these companies provide relevant volatility measures. When selecting an appropriate level of volatility for the subject company, adjustments should be considered for comparative size, growth, stage of development, profitability, and other key factors. If there is debt in the capital structure, leverage should be considered as well, although, as noted previously, this is rare for an early stage company.

- *Term.* The option-pricing model requires the expected volatility of the subject company's enterprise from the valuation date to the liquidity event date (the term). To estimate the company's expected volatility, historical indicators are often looked to as a proxy. Accordingly, the time period over which to calculate historical volatility data should be consistent with the timing to a liquidity event. For example, if the estimated term to liquidity is two years, we often look to volatility in publicly traded share prices over the historical horizon two-year period as the most relevant beginning point in deriving a proxy for expected share price volatility over the coming two years.

- *Trading volume.* The public companies selected to estimate volatility should have sufficient trading volume over the observed period to allow for accurate volatility measurement based on daily price intervals.

- *Volatility trends.* The trends of the selected public companies should be analyzed for observable mean reversion tendencies, historical trends, and cycles in their historical volatility. There are often times of extreme stock price volatility, such as that during the credit crisis of 2008 and 2009. When aberrational volatilities can be identified, it would be appropriate to make a subjective adjustment based on longer-term observable volatility.

■ *Capital structures*. The observed volatilities of public companies are based on common equity prices and, thus, demonstrate the volatilities of common equity. Since the valuation of early stage companies often includes capital structures with both common and preferred equity, an adjustment should be considered for the reduction in risk associated with preferred equity and the inclusion of both common and preferred equity in the subject company's value. It is unlikely the underlying asset, such as the company itself, would have differential volatility, but the option model clearly accords less risk to those securities that possess higher preference, such as preferred stock. Furthermore, an analysis of the public companies' leverage should be conducted and appropriate adjustments to the volatility should be made based on respective risk profiles. A more thorough discussion of this point appears in Appendix B.

Risk-Free Rate

The option-pricing model is based on risk-neutral probabilities; therefore, the discount rate reflects only the time value of money. The rate is typically based on the U.S. Treasury securities with a maturity that matches the respective term. Again, this input may require adjustment during times of aberrational financial markets, such as those during the credit crisis of 2008 and 2009.[2]

Dividend Yield

To the extent the subject company is expected to make consistent interim distributions prior to the future liquidity event date, the impact and value of these distributions can be captured through use of the dividend yield input. Often with early stage, venture-backed companies, management has no expectation to pay dividends prior to a liquidity event.

OPTION-PRICING METHOD STEPS IN APPLICATION

The key components and inputs to the option-pricing method have been outlined; now let's put them into practice. The following section provides a step-by-step example of how to apply the option-pricing method to an early stage company allocation scenario. The key steps in the application of the option-pricing method are as follows:

1. Establish the enterprise value (discussed in Chapter 3)
2. Analyze the equity rights for each class of stock to establish breakpoints (discussed in Chapter 2)
3. Select the Black-Scholes option-pricing model or the binomial model
4. Select the key valuation inputs
5. Allocate the value to the various classes of stock
6. Calculate the fair market value of the subject security

Step 1: Establishing the Enterprise Value

The enterprise value can be estimated using the traditional cost, market, or income approaches, depending on the stage and circumstances of the underlying company. As discussed in Chapter 3, there are several challenges in calculating the enterprise value for an early stage company since the subject companies are often pre-revenue and, consequently, pre-earnings. A common method for estimating the appropriate enterprise value in early stage companies is using a recent round of financing to back-solve for a company's enterprise value in a way that reconciles to the pricing of the recent financing round.

As an example, suppose you are estimating the fair market value of a minority common stock interest in new company known as Macrosecurity (the Company) for 409A purposes. Macrosecurity is an early stage software company that is in the process of developing a security software product. As of the valuation date, the Company was pre-revenue and just closed its Series A round of financing with a local VC firm for $1.0 million, or $1.00 per share. Due to the early stage of the Company, no long-term business plan forecast had been prepared. The valuation date is to be contemporaneous with the close of the financing round. The Company's capitalization as of the valuation date is as follows:

	Per-Share Issue Price	Shares Outstanding
Series A Preferred Stock	$1.00	1,000,000
Common Stock	NA	1,000,000
Total		2,000,000

In this example, we assume that the most recent transaction from the Series A financing provides the best indication of value for Macrosecurity's preferred stock. Therefore, for illustrative purposes, it is assumed that the subject company transaction method is the most appropriate method to calculate the Company's enterprise value. The enterprise value is "back-solved," or implied to result in a probability-weighted present value of the Series A preferred stock at $1.00 per share. In effect, we have used the Black-Scholes option-pricing model and have solved for the enterprise value that, given the expected term, volatility, and other inputs, results in a preferred stock value of $1.00 per share. In our example, the enterprise value is set at $1.7 million, which results in a per-share value of the Series A preferred stock of $1.00 per share, which in turn reconciles to the original purchase price. Of course, because this is an iterative process, a step-by-step linear solution cannot be performed. I present this conclusion here to contrast with the $2.0 million post-money value calculated as though all shares were worth $1.00 per share. The mechanics of reaching this conclusion are described in the following sections.

Step 2: Analyze the Equity Rights for Each Class of Stock to Establish Breakpoints

The next step is to analyze Macrosecurity's equity rights and preferences for each class of stock in order to establish the exercise prices or breakpoints in the option-pricing model. The rights and preferences of each equity class are detailed within a company's Articles of Incorporation or financing document. In the case of Macrosecurity, the following is a summary of the key sections of the Articles of Incorporation relating to the Company's equity securities.

- *Liquidation rights.* In the event of any liquidation, dissolution, or winding up of the corporation, either voluntary or involuntary, before and in preference to any distribution made to the holders of Common Stock, the holders of each share of Series A Preferred Stock shall be entitled to receive an amount per share equal to the sum of (i) $1.00 for each outstanding share of Series A Preferred Stock (the "Original Issue Price") (as adjusted for any stock dividends, combinations or splits with respect to such shares) and (ii) any declared but unpaid dividends, on each such share (in aggregate "Series A Preference").
- All of the remaining assets of this corporation available for distribution to stockholders shall be distributed ratably among the holders of

Preferred Stock and Common Stock in proportion to the number of shares of Common Stock owned by each such holder (on an as-converted to Common Stock basis) until holders of Series A Preferred Stock each receive an aggregate amount, including their Series A Preference, equal to 2.0 times the original issue price of the Series A Preferred Stock. Thereafter, the remaining assets of the Company will be distributed ratably to the holders of Common Stock.

- *Dividend rights.* Holders of Series A Preferred Stock, in preference to the holders of Common Stock, shall be entitled to receive, when, as, and if declared by the corporation's Board of Directors, but only out of funds that are legally available therefore, cash dividends at a rate of 6 percent of the Original Issue Price per annum on each outstanding share of Series A Preferred. Such dividends shall be payable only when, as, and if declared by the Board and shall not be cumulative.

- *Conversion rights.* Each share of Series A Preferred Stock shall be convertible, at the option of the holder thereof, at any time after the date of issuance of such share, into such number of fully paid and nonassessable shares of Common Stock as is determined by dividing the Original Issue Price by the Conversion Price. The initial Conversion Price per share of Series A Preferred Stock shall be the Original Issue Price.

- *Automatic conversion.* Each share of Series A Preferred Stock shall automatically be converted into shares of Common Stock at the Conversion Price at the time in effect for such share immediately upon the earlier of (i) the corporation's sale of its Common Stock in a firm commitment underwritten public offering pursuant to a registration statement under the Securities Act of 1933, as amended, in which the gross cash proceeds to the corporation are at least $30,000,000; or (ii) the date specified by written consent or agreement of the holders of a majority of the then outstanding shares of Series A Preferred Stock.

- *Voting rights.* Each holder of shares of Series A Preferred Stock shall be entitled to the number of votes equal to the number of shares of Common Stock into which such shares of Series Preferred Stock could be converted.

After discussions with management, it was determined that Macrosecurity had no plans to issue dividends prior to a liquidity event. Based on the foregoing information, Macrosecurity's capitalization and liquidation preferences are as summarized in Exhibit 4.1.

EXHIBIT 4.1 Macrosecurity's Capitalization and Liquidation Preferences

MACROSECURITY, INC.
OPTION PRICING METHOD: CAPITALIZATION

	Shares	Conversion Ratio	Fully Diluted Shares	%	Liquidation Preference per Share	Liquidation Pref. at Projected Liquidity Event	Estimated Accrued Dividends at Projected Liquidity Event	Total Liquidation Preference at Projected Liquidity Event
Series A Preferred Stock	1,000,000	1.0	1,000,000	50.0%	$ 1.00	$ 1,000,000	$ —	$ 1,000,000
Common Stock	1,000,000		1,000,000	50.0%	NA	NA	NA	NA
Total	2,000,000		2,000,000	100.0%		$ 1,000,000		$ 1,000,000

Given the rights and preferences of each class of stock, the Company's breakpoints can be calculated. Based on the foregoing information, there are three specific breakpoints for Macrosecurity. Each of these breakpoints represents a change in the distribution of assets to the common and preferred stockholders. The breakpoints are as follows:

- *Breakpoint 1.* The Series A liquidation preference. Prior to any distribution to the Common Stockholders, the Series A Preferred Stock receives its liquidation preference equal to $1.0 million. If upon a liquidity event, the enterprise value of the Company is at or below $1.0 million, then all the assets shall be distributed to the Series A Preferred Stockholders.
- *Breakpoint 2.* After the Series A Preferred Stockholders receive their liquidation preference, remaining assets are distributed to the Common Stock and Series A Preferred Stock on an as-converted *pari passu* basis until the Series A Preferred Stock reaches 2.0x its liquidation preference. The Series A Preferred Stock receives $2.0 million in aggregate at an enterprise value of $3.0 million. Upon a liquidity event, if the enterprise value of Macrosecurity is at or below $3.0 million, then the Series A Preferred Stock receives its liquidation preference and remaining assets are distributed to Series A Preferred Stock and Common Stock on a *pari passu* basis.
- *Breakpoint 3.* After the Series A Preferred Stock reaches its maximum preference at 2.0x its Original Issue Price, then all assets are distributed to Common Stock until the Series A Preferred Stock would convert to Common Stock. The Series A Preferred Stock would convert to Common Stock at an equity value of $4.0 million or more; basically, once the Common Stock receives a value of at least $2.00 per share, the Series A would be willing to convert to Common Stock. At equity values greater than $4.0 million, all shares are assumed to convert to Common Stock; therefore, assets would be distributed based on fully diluted ownership percentages.

The calculation of Macrosecurity's breakpoints is detailed in Exhibit 4.2.

Step 3: Select the Black-Scholes Option-Pricing Model or the Binomial Model

As previously mentioned, the option-pricing method involves the use of the Black-Scholes or the binomial option-pricing models. In theory,

EXHIBIT 4.2 Macrosecurity Breakpoints

MACROSECURITY, INC.
OPTION PRICING METHOD: BREAKPOINT ANALYSIS

BREAKPOINT #	Fully Diluted Shares	Percent of Total	1 Series A LP	2 Common & Preferred Stock (Series A 2 x Max)	3 Common Stock (Series A Convert)
Series A Preferred Stock	1,000,000	50.0%	$ 1,000,000	$ 1,000,000	$ —
Common Stock	1,000,000	50.0%	$ —	$ 1,000,000	$ 1,000,000
	2,000,000	100.0%			
Incremental Value (except shares)			$ 1,000,000	$ 2,000,000	$ 1,000,000
Enterprise Value Breakpoints			$ 1,000,000	$ 3,000,000	$ 4,000,000
Incremental Per Share Value[1]					
Series A Preferred Stock			$ 1.00	$ 1.00	$ —
Common Stock			$ —	$ 1.00	$ 1.00
Cumulative Per Share Value[2]					
Series A Preferred Stock			$ 1.00	$ 2.00	$ 2.00
Common Stock			$ —	$ 1.00	$ 2.00

[1]The incremental per-share value of each class of stock at each breakpoint.
[2]The cumulative per-share value of each class of stock at each breakpoint.

the solution produced by the binomial model converges to the Black-Scholes solution as the granularity of steps per period increases. Therefore, when sufficient steps are used in the binomial model and the assumptions such as term, volatility, and risk-free rate are otherwise the same, the Black-Scholes and binomial models should produce similar solutions. The following table provides some pros and cons for the use of the Black-Scholes as opposed to the binomial or lattice model.

Black-Scholes Option-Pricing Model	Binomial or Lattice Model
Often considered a "black box"	More transparency
Fast to calculate	More flexibility
Not flexible	Complex to build

As mentioned previously, the binomial model provides more transparency and flexibility than the Black-Scholes model. It allows the user to see each of the expected exit values at the time of the liquidity event and allocate the distributable assets to each class of stock in a similar fashion to the scenario-based or probability-weighted expected-return method. Each of the exit events is treated as a separate scenario outcome, and assets can be distributed accordingly. This level of transparency provides the user with greater flexibility to alter the allocation of proceeds, if necessary; it also helps provide more insight into the magnitude of discounts to apply. For example, if the subject company's most likely liquidity event is an IPO and the automatic conversion feature of the preferred stock would be triggered, the lattice, or binomial, model allows the user to determine at each exit event value whether the automatic conversion feature is triggered and whether assets should be allocated assuming automatic conversion of the preferred stock. The Black-Scholes model does not allow for this level of transparency and flexibility. However, given its advantages and disadvantages, in practice, the Black-Scholes model is far more commonly used. The facts and circumstances unique to each valuation should be considered when selecting the appropriate option-pricing model for each engagement.

The analyst should keep in mind when utilizing these option-pricing models that they were not created specifically for use in allocating value among the equity classes of early stage companies. Fisher Black would probably turn over in his grave if he knew what practitioners are doing with his model! Although these option models are used in practice, the analyst should be aware of their limitations, which are discussed at the end of this chapter. For Macrosecurity, we demonstrate both the Black-Scholes and lattice option models simultaneously for illustrative purposes.

Step 4: Select the Key Valuation Inputs

The key inputs for the Black-Scholes and the binomial models are detailed in the following list and in Exhibit 4.3 for Macrosecurity:

- *Underlying asset value.* The underlying asset value used in the option-pricing method is the Company's enterprise value. In the case of Macrosecurity, this is based on the implied equity value that results in a probability-weighted present value for the Series A preferred stock of $1.00 per share. The Company's equity value that results in an allocated value to the Series A preferred stock of $1.00 per share is $1.7 million.

EXHIBIT 4.3   Black-Scholes Option-Pricing Model Inputs

MACROSECURITY, INC.
MODIFIED BLACK-SCHOLES
OPTION PRICING MODEL: KEY INPUTS

Assumptions

Underlying Asset Value:	$ 1,700,954
Term (Years):	5.0
Date of Valuation:	12/31/2008
Date of Liquidity Event:	12/31/2013
Risk-Free Rate:	1.55%
Volatility:	90.00%
Dividend Yield:	0.00%
Exercise Prices (Breakpoints):	

No.	Breakpoint Description	Exercise Price
1	NA	$ —
2	Series A LP	$ 1,000,000
3	Common & Preferred Stock (Series A 2× Max)	$ 3,000,000
4	Common Stock (Series A Convert)	$ 4,000,000

- *Exercise price.* The exercise prices should correspond to the breakpoint analysis described in the section headed Step 2. The first exercise price is always $0.00, resulting in the option value of the entire enterprise (this represents the entire value available to allocate to the preferred and common stock). The second exercise price is equal to the liquidation preference of the preferred stock (breakpoint 1). Each successive breakpoint is modeled until all of the preferred stock's attributes are addressed.
- *Term.* Term is based on discussion with management and supplemental analysis of the company's position, industry, and market. A five-year term is estimated as the most likely timing for a liquidity event for Macrosecurity.
- *Volatility.* Volatility is based on selected public companies operating in the security software space, in addition to supplemental analysis. We estimated the expected volatility for Macrosecurity over a five-year horizon period at 90 percent.
- *Risk-free rate.* The risk-free rate is based on the five-year Treasury security as of the valuation date at 1.55 percent.
- *Dividend yield.* According to management, the Company has no expectation to issue dividends prior to a liquidity event. Therefore, the dividend yield is 0 percent.

Binomial or Lattice Model Inputs For Macrosecurity, we selected a lattice of enterprise value outcomes calculated based on 36 periods—that is, 36 steps of upward and downward movements in the enterprise value. The upward and downward movements are based on the time increments and volatility. Shown in Exhibit 4.7 is the example of the lattice for Macrosecurity as an interim step in the overall valuation process.

Step 5: Allocate Value to the Various Classes of Stock

The modeled proceeds are distributed to the preferred stock and common stock based on their respective rights and preferences as detailed in the breakpoint analysis. The primary difference between the Black-Scholes option-pricing model and the binomial model is that in Black-Scholes, the probability-weighted present value of the payoffs to the equity classes is allocated within the formula; under the binomial model, the distributable proceeds are allocated directly to the equity classes as discrete outputs.

EXHIBIT 4.4   Lattice for Macrosecurity

ASSUMPTIONS

	Annual	Per Period	
Underlying Stock Price ($M):		$ 1.70	
Term:		5.00	
Number for Periods:		**36 Periods**	
Periods per Year (Pr):		7	
Volatility (σ):	90.00%	33.54%	$= \sigma \times \sqrt{(1/Pr)}$
Risk-Free Rate (Rf):	1.55%	0.22%	$= EXP(Rf)^{\wedge}(1/Pr) - 1$
Movement Up (Mu):		1.3985	$= EXP(\sigma_{per\,Period})$
Movement Down (Md):		0.7150	$= 1 / Mu$
Probability Up (Pu):		42.01%	$= ((Rf_{per\,period} + 1) - Md)/ (Mu - Md)$
Probability Down (Pd):		57.99%	$= 1 - Pu$

Black-Scholes Option-Pricing Model Allocation   As shown in Exhibit 4.5, the Black-Scholes inputs are run through the model to determine the value of the call option at each breakpoint. Each follow-on option is then deducted from the prior period call option to determine the incremental option value. This incremental option value is then allocated based on the modeled allocations of the preferred and common participatory rights. The aggregate value of the allocated proceeds is then divided by the total number of outstanding, shares of each share class to arrive at a per-share value for each share class. As noted at the beginning of this example, the preferred stock price is "optioned" to equal the issue price—$1.00 in this case—of the latest round of financing.

The payoff to the common and preferred stock can also be represented in an option payoff chart, as shown in Exhibit 4.6. The visual graphic allows for an easier presentation of the discrete payoffs between the various equity classes.

Binomial Option Model Allocation   The binomial option model uses the same breakpoints as the Black-Scholes option-pricing model to allocate the future exit event proceeds to the various classes of stock. In the following example, period 36 represents the various potential exit event values at the liquidity event in year five. (Holding all other inputs equal, increasing or decreasing the number of periods has little impact on the per-share value of the preferred and common stock over a short period of time.) At each

EXHIBIT 4.5 Black-Scholes Option-Pricing Model Valuation

MACROSECURITY, INC.
MODIFIED BLACK-SCHOLES OPTION PRICING MODEL: OPTION VALUATION & ALLOCATION

Black-Scholes Option Model Valuation

	1	2	3	End
Black-Scholes Inputs				
Firm Value @ Valuation Date	$ 1,700,954	$ 1,700,954	$ 1,700,954	$1,700,954
Breakpoints	—	1,000,000	3,000,000	4,000,000
Dividend Yield	0.00%	0.00%	0.00%	0.00%
Years to Maturity	5.00	5.00	5.00	5.00
Risk-Free Rate (Rf)	1.55%	1.55%	1.55%	1.55%
Volatility	90.00%	90.00%	90.00%	90.00%
Value of Call Option	$ 1,700,954	$ 1,315,988	$ 1,028,511	$ 942,591
Follow-on Option	$(1,315,988)	$(1,028,511)	$ (942,591)	$ —
Incremental Option Value	$ 384,966	$ 287,477	$ 85,919	$ 942,591

(Continued)

EXHIBIT 4.5 (*Continued*)

Option Value Allocation

% of Incremental Option Value	1	2	3	End
Series A Preferred Stock	100.0%	50.0%	0.0%	50.0%
Common Stock	0.0%	50.0%	100.0%	50.0%
Total	100%	100%	100%	100%

Incremental Option Value	1	2	3	End	Aggregate Equity Value	Shares	Per-Share Value
Series A Preferred Stock	$ 384,966	$ 143,739	$ —	$ 471,296	$ 1,000,000	1,000,000	$ 1.00
Common Stock	$ —	$ 143,739	$ 85,919	$ 471,296	$ 700,954	1,000,000	$ 0.70
Total	$ 384,966	$ 287,477	$ 85,919	$ 942,591	$ 1,700,954	2,000,000	

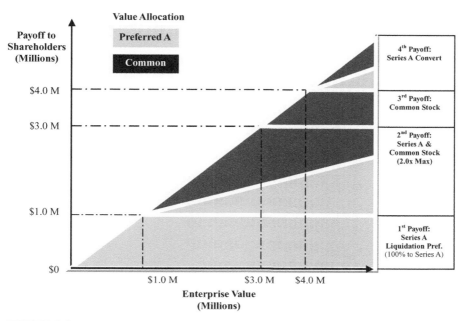

EXHIBIT 4.6   Payoff to Common and Preferred Shareholders under a Liquidity Event

of those potential exit scenarios, the future proceeds are allocated to the Series A and common stock, based on the breakpoint analysis. This demonstrates the point made previously regarding the discrete allocations under the binomial option model as opposed to the "black box" allocation of the Black-Scholes model.

Note in Exhibit 4.7 that the preferred and common stock share on an as-converted *pari passu* basis at most valuation levels. It is only when the overall end node value drops below the 17th level do the preferred and common values diverge. When this phenomenon occurs, it is referred to as a "common-friendly" capital structure because the common stock values, pre-discount, are quite close to the original issue preferred price. Take away the 2x participation attribute of the preferred, and the share values become even more similar.

In order to assess the specific allocations to each share class, the present value of the Series A preferred stock and common stock is calculated based on the allocation in period 36 and the present value discount rate. The future allocated proceeds for each share class end up within period 36 of the lattice model, and the model probability weights and present values those future proceeds back to the valuation date to determine the indicated value of each class of stock, as shown in Exhibits 4.8 and 4.9. Note the extremely

0	1	2	3	4	5	6	7	8	9	10	11	12	13	14	15	16	17	18	19	20	21	22	23	24	25	26	27	28	29	30	31	32	33	34	35	36	36		Allocation	
																																							Series A	Common Stock
																																					298,330.16	149,165.08	149,165.08
																																					152,532.92	76,266.46	76,266.46
$1.75	2.38	3.33	4.65	6.51	9.10	12.73	17.80	24.89	34.81	48.68	68.06	95.21	133.16	186.22	260.43	364.22	509.36	712.35	996.23	1,393.25	1,948.48	2,724.97	3,810.91	5,329.61	7,453.54	10,423.87	14,577.93	20,387.44	28,512.12	39,874.60	55,785.19	77,988.39	109,067.86	152,532.92	213,319.41	298,330.16	77,988.39	38,994.20	38,994.20
	1.22	1.70	2.38	3.33	4.65	6.51	9.10	12.73	17.80	24.89	34.81	48.68	68.06	95.21	133.16	186.22	260.43	364.22	509.36	712.35	996.23	1,393.25	1,948.48	2,724.97	3,810.91	5,329.61	7,453.54	10,423.87	14,577.93	20,387.44	28,512.12	39,874.60	55,785.19	77,988.39	109,067.86	152,532.92	39,874.60	19,937.30	19,937.30
		0.87	1.22	1.70	2.38	3.33	4.65	6.51	9.10	12.73	17.80	24.89	34.81	48.68	68.08	95.21	133.16	186.22	260.43	364.22	509.36	712.35	996.23	1,393.25	1,948.48	2,724.97	3,810.91	5,329.61	7,453.54	10,423.87	14,577.93	20,387.44	28,512.12	39,874.60	55,785.19	77,988.39	20,387.44	10,193.72	10,193.72
			0.62	0.87	1.22	1.70	2.38	3.33	4.65	6.51	9.10	12.73	17.80	24.89	34.81	48.68	68.08	95.21	133.16	186.22	260.43	364.22	509.36	712.35	996.23	1,393.25	1,948.48	2,724.97	3,810.91	5,329.61	7,453.54	10,423.87	14,577.93	20,387.44	28,512.12	39,874.60	10,423.87	5,211.94	5,211.94
				0.44	0.62	0.87	1.22	1.70	2.38	3.33	4.65	6.51	9.10	12.73	17.80	24.89	34.81	48.68	68.06	95.21	133.16	186.22	260.43	364.22	509.36	712.35	996.23	1,393.25	1,948.48	2,724.97	3,810.91	5,329.61	7,453.54	10,423.87	14,577.93	20,387.44	5,329.61	2,664.81	2,664.81
					0.32	0.44	0.62	0.87	1.22	1.70	2.38	3.33	4.65	6.51	9.10	12.73	17.80	24.89	34.81	48.68	68.08	95.21	133.16	186.22	260.43	364.22	509.36	712.35	996.23	1,393.25	1,948.48	2,724.97	3,810.91	5,329.61	7,453.54	10,423.87	2,724.97	1,362.49	1,362.49
						0.23	0.32	0.44	0.62	0.87	1.22	1.70	2.38	3.33	4.65	6.51	9.10	12.73	17.80	24.89	34.81	48.68	68.08	95.21	133.16	186.22	260.43	364.22	509.36	712.35	996.23	1,393.25	1,948.48	2,724.97	3,810.91	5,329.61	1,393.25	696.62	696.62
							0.16	0.23	0.32	0.44	0.62	0.87	1.22	1.70	2.38	3.33	4.65	6.51	9.10	12.73	17.80	24.89	34.81	48.68	68.08	95.21	133.16	186.22	260.43	364.22	509.36	712.35	996.23	1,393.25	1,948.48	2,724.97	712.35	356.18	356.18
								0.12	0.16	0.23	0.32	0.44	0.62	0.87	1.22	1.70	2.38	3.33	4.65	6.51	9.10	12.73	17.80	24.89	34.81	48.68	68.08	95.21	133.16	186.22	260.43	364.22	509.36	712.35	996.23	1,393.25	364.22	182.11	182.11
									0.08	0.12	0.16	0.23	0.32	0.44	0.62	0.87	1.22	1.70	2.38	3.33	4.65	6.51	9.10	12.73	17.80	24.89	34.81	48.68	68.08	95.21	133.16	186.22	260.43	364.22	509.36	712.35	186.22	93.11	93.11
										0.06	0.08	0.12	0.16	0.23	0.32	0.44	0.62	0.87	1.22	1.70	2.38	3.33	4.65	6.51	9.10	12.73	17.80	24.89	34.81	48.68	68.08	95.21	133.16	186.22	260.43	364.22	95.21	47.61	47.61
											0.04	0.06	0.08	0.12	0.16	0.23	0.32	0.44	0.62	0.87	1.22	1.70	2.38	3.33	4.65	6.51	9.10	12.73	17.80	24.89	34.81	48.68	68.08	95.21	133.16	186.22	48.68	24.34	24.34
												0.03	0.04	0.06	0.08	0.12	0.16	0.23	0.32	0.44	0.62	0.87	1.22	1.70	2.38	3.33	4.65	6.51	9.10	12.73	17.80	24.89	34.81	48.68	68.08	95.21	24.89	12.45	12.45
													0.02	0.03	0.04	0.06	0.08	0.12	0.16	0.23	0.32	0.44	0.62	0.87	1.22	1.70	2.38	3.33	4.65	6.51	9.10	12.73	17.80	24.89	34.81	48.68	12.73	6.36	6.36
														0.02	0.02	0.03	0.04	0.06	0.08	0.12	0.16	0.23	0.32	0.44	0.62	0.87	1.22	1.70	2.38	3.33	4.65	6.51	9.10	12.73	17.80	24.89	6.51	3.25	3.25
															0.01	0.02	0.02	0.03	0.04	0.06	0.08	0.12	0.16	0.23	0.32	0.44	0.62	0.87	1.22	1.70	2.38	3.33	4.65	6.51	9.10	12.73	3.33	2.00	1.33
																0.01	0.01	0.02	0.02	0.03	0.04	0.06	0.08	0.12	0.16	0.23	0.32	0.44	0.62	0.87	1.22	1.70	2.38	3.33	4.65	6.51	1.70	1.35	0.35
																0.00	0.01	0.01	0.02	0.02	0.03	0.04	0.06	0.08	0.12	0.16	0.23	0.32	0.44	0.62	0.87	1.22	1.70	2.38	3.33	4.65	0.87	0.87	–
																	0.00	0.00	0.01	0.01	0.01	0.02	0.03	0.04	0.06	0.08	0.12	0.16	0.23	0.32	0.44	0.62	0.87	1.22	1.70	2.38	0.44	0.44	–
																		0.00	0.00	0.01	0.01	0.01	0.02	0.02	0.03	0.04	0.06	0.08	0.12	0.16	0.23	0.32	0.44	0.62	0.87	1.22	0.23	0.23	–
																			0.00	0.00	0.00	0.01	0.01	0.01	0.02	0.02	0.03	0.04	0.06	0.08	0.12	0.16	0.23	0.32	0.44	0.62	0.12	0.12	–
																				0.00	0.00	0.00	0.00	0.01	0.01	0.01	0.02	0.02	0.03	0.04	0.06	0.08	0.12	0.16	0.23	0.32	0.06	0.06	–
																					0.00	0.00	0.00	0.00	0.01	0.01	0.01	0.02	0.02	0.03	0.04	0.06	0.08	0.12	0.16	0.23	0.03	0.03	–
																						0.00	0.00	0.00	0.00	0.01	0.01	0.01	0.02	0.02	0.03	0.04	0.06	0.08	0.12	0.16	0.02	0.02	–
																							0.00	0.00	0.00	0.00	0.01	0.01	0.01	0.02	0.02	0.03	0.04	0.06	0.08	0.12	0.01	0.01	–
																								0.00	0.00	0.00	0.00	0.01	0.01	0.01	0.02	0.02	0.03	0.04	0.06	0.08	0.00	0.00	–
																									0.00	0.00	0.00	0.00	0.01	0.01	0.01	0.02	0.02	0.03	0.04	0.06	0.00	0.00	–
																										0.00	0.00	0.00	0.00	0.01	0.01	0.01	0.02	0.02	0.03	0.04	0.00	0.00	–
																											0.00	0.00	0.00	0.00	0.01	0.01	0.01	0.02	0.02	0.03	0.00	0.00	–
																												0.00	0.00	0.00	0.00	0.01	0.01	0.01	0.02	0.02	0.00	0.00	–
																													0.00	0.00	0.00	0.00	0.01	0.01	0.01	0.02	0.00	0.00	–
																														0.00	0.00	0.00	0.00	0.01	0.01	0.01	0.00	0.00	–
																															0.00	0.00	0.00	0.00	0.01	0.01	0.00	0.00	–

EXHIBIT 4.7   Preferred and Common Stock Allocation

high 36-period value generated by the lattice model, $149,165,080,000! The math, of course, is simple; each successive period is increased by the calculated movement up for 36 periods. The binomial model is telling us that if the company's value moves up for 36 successive periods over five years, based on an annual volatility of 90 percent, Macrosecurity's aggregate value would reach a lofty $298,330,160,000 (twice the value of the individual security classes noted earlier), although the probability of this ocurring is virtually zero. Just for fun, if the Company's volatility is decreased to 45 percent, the aggregate enterprise drops to a mere $712,350,000, but the per-share prices for preferred and common change only to $1.15 and $0.55, respectively, instead of the $1.00 and $0.70 share prices at 90 percent volatility. After observing the aggregate company values generated at the high end discretely through the binomial model, the analyst should question the reliability of the outputs. A review of the following tables, however, does reveal that over 75 percent probability of the potential outcomes indicate no value for the common stock. Understanding the range of values generated by option models helps to place the overall valuation exercise in context.

Step 6: Calculate the Fair Market Value of the Subject Security

The total allocated values to each class of stock, before applicable discounts, based on the Black-Scholes and binomial models, are as follows:

BLACK-SCHOLES

	Total Allocated Value	Total Shares	Per-Share Value
Series A Preferred Stock	$ 1,000,000	1,000,000	$ 1.00
Common Stock	$ 700,954	1,000,000	$ 0.70

BINOMIAL 36 PERIODS

	Total Allocated Value	Total Shares	Per-Share Value
Series A Preferred Stock	$ 1,001,644	1,000,000	$ 1.00
Common Stock	$ 699,168	1,000,000	$ 0.70

BINOMIAL SOLUTION TREE: SERIES A PREFERRED STOCK ($000,000's)

	0	1	2	3	4	5	6	7	8	9	10	11	12	13	14	15	16	17	18	19	20	21
	$1.00	1.36	1.85	2.52	3.45	4.75	6.56	9.08	12.60	17.54	24.44	34.12	47.66	66.61	93.12	130.22	182.10	254.67	356.16	498.10	696.60	974.20
		0.75	1.01	1.37	1.86	2.53	3.46	4.75	6.56	9.07	12.60	17.53	24.43	34.11	47.65	66.60	93.12	130.22	182.10	254.67	356.16	498.10
			0.56	0.75	1.02	1.37	1.86	2.54	3.47	4.76	6.56	9.07	12.59	17.52	24.42	34.10	47.64	66.59	93.11	130.21	182.10	254.67
				0.42	0.57	0.76	1.03	1.38	1.87	2.54	3.47	4.76	6.56	9.07	12.58	17.51	24.41	34.08	47.63	66.59	93.11	130.21
					0.32	0.43	0.57	0.77	1.03	1.39	1.88	2.55	3.48	4.76	6.55	9.06	12.57	17.50	24.40	34.07	47.62	66.58
						0.24	0.32	0.43	0.58	0.78	1.04	1.40	1.89	2.56	3.48	4.76	6.55	9.05	12.56	17.48	24.39	34.06
							0.18	0.24	0.33	0.44	0.59	0.79	1.05	1.41	1.90	2.57	3.49	4.76	6.54	9.04	12.55	17.47
								0.14	0.18	0.25	0.33	0.45	0.60	0.80	1.07	1.42	1.91	2.57	3.49	4.76	6.54	9.03
									0.10	0.14	0.19	0.25	0.34	0.46	0.61	0.81	1.08	1.44	1.92	2.58	3.49	4.76
										0.08	0.10	0.14	0.19	0.26	0.35	0.46	0.62	0.82	1.09	1.45	1.93	2.59
											0.06	0.08	0.11	0.14	0.19	0.26	0.35	0.47	0.63	0.84	1.11	1.46
												0.04	0.06	0.08	0.11	0.15	0.20	0.27	0.36	0.48	0.64	0.85
													0.03	0.04	0.06	0.08	0.11	0.15	0.20	0.27	0.37	0.49
														0.02	0.04	0.04	0.06	0.08	0.11	0.15	0.21	0.28
															0.02	0.02	0.03	0.04	0.06	0.08	0.11	0.15
																0.01	0.02	0.02	0.03	0.04	0.06	0.08
																	0.01	0.01	0.02	0.02	0.03	0.04
																			0.01	0.01	0.02	0.02
																			0.00	0.01	0.01	0.01
																				0.00	0.00	0.01
																					0.00	0.00
																						0.00

22	23	24	25	26	27	28	29	30	31	32	33	34	35	36
1,362.44	1,905.40	2,664.73	3,726.67	5,211.82	7,288.82	10,193.53	14,255.83	19,937.02	27,882.27	38,993.84	54,533.55	76,266.10	106,659.46	149,165.08
696.60	974.21	1,362.45	1,905.41	2,664.74	3,726.69	5,211.84	7,288.85	10,193.58	14,255.90	19,937.12	27,882.40	38,994.02	54,533.80	76,266.46
356.16	498.10	696.60	974.21	1,362.45	1,905.42	2,664.76	3,726.71	5,211.86	7,288.88	10,193.63	14,255.96	19,937.21	27,882.53	38,994.20
182.10	254.67	356.17	498.10	696.61	974.22	1,362.46	1,905.42	2,664.77	3,726.73	5,211.89	7,288.92	10,193.67	14,256.03	19,937.30
93.11	130.21	182.10	254.68	356.17	498.11	696.61	974.22	1,362.47	1,905.43	2,664.78	3,726.74	5,211.91	7,288.95	10,193.72
47.61	66.58	93.11	130.21	182.10	254.68	356.17	498.11	696.61	974.23	1,362.47	1,905.44	2,664.79	3,726.76	5,211.94
24.38	34.06	47.61	66.58	93.11	130.21	182.11	254.68	356.17	498.11	696.62	974.23	1,362.48	1,905.45	2,664.81
12.53	17.45	24.36	34.05	47.61	66.58	93.11	130.21	182.11	254.68	356.17	498.11	696.62	974.24	1,362.49
6.53	9.01	12.51	17.44	24.35	34.04	47.61	66.58	93.11	130.21	182.11	254.68	356.17	498.12	696.62
3.49	4.75	6.51	8.99	12.50	17.42	24.34	34.04	47.61	66.58	93.11	130.22	182.11	254.68	356.18
1.94	2.59	3.49	4.74	6.49	8.97	12.48	17.41	24.34	34.04	47.61	66.58	93.11	130.22	182.11
1.12	1.48	1.95	2.60	3.48	4.72	6.47	8.95	12.46	17.40	24.34	34.04	47.61	66.58	93.11
0.66	0.87	1.14	1.50	1.97	2.60	3.47	4.69	6.44	8.92	12.44	17.40	24.34	34.04	47.61
0.38	0.51	0.67	0.89	1.16	1.51	1.98	2.60	3.45	4.66	6.40	8.90	12.44	17.40	24.34
0.21	0.29	0.39	0.52	0.69	0.91	1.19	1.54	1.99	2.59	3.42	4.62	6.36	8.90	12.45
0.11	0.16	0.21	0.29	0.40	0.54	0.71	0.94	1.21	1.56	1.99	2.56	3.37	4.55	6.36
0.06	0.08	0.11	0.16	0.22	0.30	0.41	0.55	0.74	0.97	1.25	1.59	1.99	2.52	3.25
0.03	0.04	0.06	0.08	0.12	0.16	0.22	0.31	0.42	0.57	0.77	1.01	1.30	1.62	2.00
0.02	0.02	0.03	0.04	0.06	0.08	0.12	0.16	0.23	0.31	0.43	0.60	0.81	1.07	1.35
0.01	0.01	0.02	0.02	0.03	0.04	0.06	0.08	0.12	0.16	0.23	0.32	0.44	0.62	0.87
0.00	0.01	0.01	0.01	0.02	0.02	0.03	0.04	0.06	0.08	0.12	0.16	0.23	0.32	0.44
0.00	0.00	0.00	0.01	0.01	0.01	0.02	0.02	0.03	0.04	0.06	0.08	0.12	0.16	0.23
0.00	0.00	0.00	0.00	0.00	0.01	0.01	0.01	0.02	0.02	0.03	0.04	0.06	0.08	0.12
		0.00	0.00	0.00	0.00	0.00	0.00	0.01	0.01	0.02	0.02	0.03	0.04	0.06
		0.00		0.00	0.00	0.00	0.00	0.00	0.01	0.01	0.01	0.02	0.02	0.03
						0.00	0.00	0.00	0.00	0.00	0.01	0.01	0.01	0.02
							0.00	0.00	0.00	0.00	0.00	0.00	0.00	0.01
								0.00	0.00	0.00	0.00	0.00	0.00	0.00
									0.00	0.00	0.00	0.00	0.00	0.00
										0.00	0.00	0.00	0.00	0.00
											0.00	0.00	0.00	0.00
													0.00	0.00
													0.00	0.00
														0.00
														0.00

EXHIBIT 4.8 Binomial Solution Tree: Series A Preferred Stock

BINOMIAL SOLUTION TREE: COMMON STOCK ($000,000's)

0	1	2	3	4	5	6	7	8	9	10	11	12	13	14	15	16	17	18	19	20	21
$ 0.70	1.02	1.48	2.13	3.05	4.35	6.17	8.72	12.29	17.27	24.24	33.96	47.55	66.54	93.09	130.20	182.10	254.67	356.16	498.10	696.60	974.20
	0.47	0.69	1.01	1.47	2.12	3.05	4.35	6.17	8.72	12.29	17.28	24.24	33.97	47.56	66.55	93.09	130.20	182.10	254.67	356.16	498.10
		0.31	0.46	0.68	1.00	1.46	2.12	3.04	4.34	6.17	8.73	12.30	17.29	24.25	33.98	47.57	66.56	93.10	130.21	182.10	254.67
			0.20	0.30	0.45	0.68	1.00	1.45	2.11	3.03	4.34	6.17	8.73	12.31	17.30	24.27	33.99	47.58	66.56	93.10	130.21
				0.13	0.19	0.30	0.45	0.67	0.99	1.45	2.10	3.03	4.34	6.17	8.74	12.32	17.31	24.28	34.00	47.59	66.57
					0.08	0.12	0.19	0.29	0.44	0.66	0.98	1.44	2.09	3.03	4.34	6.18	8.74	12.33	17.32	24.29	34.01
						0.05	0.07	0.12	0.18	0.28	0.43	0.65	0.97	1.43	2.09	3.02	4.34	6.18	8.75	12.34	17.34
							0.03	0.04	0.07	0.11	0.17	0.27	0.42	0.64	0.95	1.42	2.08	3.02	4.34	6.19	8.77
								0.01	0.02	0.04	0.06	0.10	0.17	0.26	0.41	0.62	0.94	1.41	2.07	3.02	4.34
									0.01	0.01	0.02	0.04	0.06	0.10	0.16	0.25	0.39	0.61	0.93	1.40	2.07
										0.00	0.01	0.01	0.02	0.03	0.05	0.09	0.15	0.24	0.38	0.60	0.92
											0.00	0.00	0.01	0.01	0.02	0.03	0.05	0.08	0.14	0.23	0.37
												0.00	0.00	0.00	0.00	0.01	0.01	0.02	0.04	0.08	0.13
													0.00	0.00	0.00	0.00	0.00	0.01	0.01	0.02	0.04
														0.00	0.00	0.00	0.00	0.00	0.00	0.00	0.01
															0.00	0.00	0.00	0.00	0.00	0.00	0.00
																0.00	0.00	0.00	0.00	0.00	0.00
																	0.00	0.00	0.00	0.00	0.00
																		0.00	0.00	0.00	0.00
																			0.00	0.00	0.00
																				0.00	0.00
																					0.00

	22	23	24	25	26	27	28	29	30	31	32	33	34	35	36
	1,362.44	1,905.40	2,664.73	3,726.67	5,211.82	7,288.82	10,193.53	14,255.83	19,937.02	27,882.27	38,993.84	54,533.55	76,266.10	106,659.46	149,165.08
	696.60	974.21	1,362.45	1,905.41	2,664.74	3,726.69	5,211.84	7,288.85	10,193.58	14,255.90	19,937.12	27,882.40	38,994.02	54,533.80	76,266.46
	356.16	498.10	696.60	974.21	1,362.45	1,905.42	2,664.76	3,726.71	5,211.86	7,288.88	10,193.63	14,255.96	19,937.21	27,882.53	38,994.20
	182.10	254.67	356.17	498.10	696.61	974.22	1,362.48	1,905.42	2,664.77	3,726.73	5,211.89	7,288.92	10,193.67	14,256.03	19,937.30
	93.11	130.21	182.10	254.68	356.17	498.11	696.61	974.22	1,362.47	1,905.43	2,664.78	3,726.74	5,211.91	7,288.95	10,193.72
	47.59	66.57	93.11	130.21	182.10	254.68	356.17	498.11	696.61	974.23	1,362.47	1,905.44	2,664.79	3,726.76	5,211.94
	24.30	34.02	47.60	66.58	93.11	130.21	182.11	254.68	356.17	498.11	696.62	974.23	1,362.48	1,905.45	2,664.81
	12.36	17.35	24.32	34.03	47.60	66.58	93.11	130.21	182.11	254.68	356.17	498.11	696.62	974.24	1,362.49
	6.20	8.78	12.37	17.37	24.33	34.04	47.61	66.58	93.11	130.21	182.11	254.68	356.17	498.12	696.62
	3.02	4.35	6.22	8.80	12.39	17.38	24.34	34.04	47.61	66.58	93.11	130.22	182.11	254.68	356.18
	1.38	2.06	3.02	4.36	6.23	8.83	12.41	17.40	24.34	34.04	47.61	66.58	93.11	130.22	182.11
	0.58	0.90	1.37	2.06	3.02	4.38	6.26	8.85	12.43	17.40	24.34	34.04	47.61	66.58	93.11
	0.21	0.35	0.56	0.88	1.36	2.05	3.04	4.40	6.29	8.86	12.44	17.40	24.34	34.04	47.61
	0.07	0.12	0.20	0.33	0.54	0.86	1.35	2.06	3.06	4.44	6.33	8.90	12.44	17.40	24.34
	0.02	0.03	0.06	0.10	0.18	0.31	0.52	0.84	1.34	2.07	3.09	4.48	6.36	8.90	12.45
	0.00	0.01	0.01	0.02	0.05	0.09	0.16	0.28	0.49	0.82	1.33	2.09	3.14	4.55	6.36
	0.00	0.00	0.00	0.00	0.01	0.02	0.03	0.07	0.13	0.25	0.45	0.79	1.33	2.13	3.25
	0.00	0.00	0.00	0.00	0.00	0.00	0.00	0.01	0.02	0.05	0.10	0.20	0.40	0.76	1.33
	0.00	0.00	0.00	0.00	0.00	0.00	0.00	0.00	0.00	0.00	0.01	0.03	0.06	0.15	0.35
	0.00	0.00	0.00	0.00	0.00	0.00	0.00	0.00	0.00	0.00	0.00	0.00	0.00	0.00	0.00
	0.00	0.00	0.00	0.00	0.00	0.00	0.00	0.00	0.00	0.00	0.00	0.00	0.00	0.00	0.00
	0.00	0.00	0.00	0.00	0.00	0.00	0.00	0.00	0.00	0.00	0.00	0.00	0.00	0.00	0.00
	0.00	0.00	0.00	0.00	0.00	0.00	0.00	0.00	0.00	0.00	0.00	0.00	0.00	0.00	0.00
		0.00	0.00	0.00	0.00	0.00	0.00	0.00	0.00	0.00	0.00	0.00	0.00	0.00	0.00
			0.00	0.00	0.00	0.00	0.00	0.00	0.00	0.00	0.00	0.00	0.00	0.00	0.00
				0.00	0.00	0.00	0.00	0.00	0.00	0.00	0.00	0.00	0.00	0.00	0.00
					0.00	0.00	0.00	0.00	0.00	0.00	0.00	0.00	0.00	0.00	0.00
						0.00	0.00	0.00	0.00	0.00	0.00	0.00	0.00	0.00	0.00
							0.00	0.00	0.00	0.00	0.00	0.00	0.00	0.00	0.00
								0.00	0.00	0.00	0.00	0.00	0.00	0.00	0.00
									0.00	0.00	0.00	0.00	0.00	0.00	0.00
										0.00	0.00	0.00	0.00	0.00	0.00
											0.00	0.00	0.00	0.00	0.00
												0.00	0.00	0.00	0.00
													0.00	0.00	0.00
														0.00	0.00
															0.00

EXHIBIT 4.9 Binomial Solution Tree: Common Stock

The per-share values derived in the foregoing examples are "raw" in that they represent contractually allocated values of Macrosecurity's aggregate equity. In order to derive the "fair market value" of the common stock (i.e., the price a willing buyer would pay to step into the shoes of the current common stockholder), appropriate premiums and discounts must be considered and, if applicable, applied to the common stock. (The selection of the appropriate discounts is discussed in more detail in Chapter 6.) For the purposes of this example, it is assumed that only a discount for lack of marketability is appropriate for the common stock. For illustrative purposes only, a 50 percent discount is applied to the aggregate value of the common stock as determined by the option-pricing models.

Indicated Value of Common Stock per Share		$ 0.70
Less Discount for Lack of Marketability	50%	$ (0.35)
Fair Market Value of Common Stock Per Share		$ 0.35

OTHER CONSIDERATIONS IN THE OPTION-PRICING METHOD

As previously mentioned, the option-pricing method is based on a forward-looking premise. Essentially, the key in valuing common shares in an early stage company is to match the future shares outstanding to the future value; therefore, the expected capitalization structure at the time of an exit event must be estimated. Given this requirement, the valuation analyst must often deal with other complexities, such as the potential dilution in common stock value arising from (1) potential new financing rounds and (2) potential issuance of additional common stock options.

- *Future financing rounds.* If there is a high likelihood of a future financing round, the analyst can factor this future financing round directly into the model by estimating the timing of the round, the dollar amount of the round, and the number of common stock equivalents to be issued from the financing. This is usually accomplished by relying on management's estimates as to timing, amount, and terms of the financing, and by extrapolating, via the option model, the estimated per-share value at the future financing date. This factor is discussed further in Chapter 7.

- *Option exercise.* In early stage companies, there is often a large pool of options that have yet to be granted. Due to the potential dilutive impact of the option pool, the amount of the option pool expected to be granted prior to a liquidity event should be included within the analysis. Again, this is typically accomplished through discussions with management and understanding employee hiring expectations. And don't forget option proceeds! If the option is assumed to exercise, the impact of option proceeds on the overall value of the company must be considered. Although most likely immaterial, it is value nonetheless; however, it is typically captured in the option pricing method through the breakpoint selections.

PROS AND CONS OF THE OPTION-PRICING METHOD

In my experience, the option-pricing method is the allocation model most commonly employed by practitioners, and it is often preferred by accounting firms that review independent third-party valuations. Accounting professionals like the option model because there are a limited number of inputs, which can be audited and tested much more readily than with other allocation models. This is not to say the option model is superior or always accurate, but rather that the inputs are easy to identify. Furthermore, the option-pricing model can be more appropriate than a scenario-based allocation model when the timing, type, and values of the future exit event outcomes cannot be reasonably estimated. Another positive (or negative depending on your perspective) of the option-pricing method is that it always attributes some value to the common stock, even if it doesn't have value under the current value method. However, this is also true of the discrete scenario method.

The pitfalls of the option-pricing method are related to its limitations. The option-pricing model was not created for the valuation of early stage companies, so its application to the valuation of such companies is strained. It's not that it can't be used, but don't forget my admonition that you need to know and understand the rules so that you can break them if needed. In addition to the structural problems of the option model, future value outcomes may not be (and normally are not) lognormally distributed (sorry about the pun). As such, the option-pricing method may not fully capture the high likelihood of failure (we already witnessed the model's ability to generate incredulous upside value).

In addition, since the option-pricing method implies some residual value to the option holder, this concept has been questioned by company owners and board members, who argue that their company is extremely risky and that the common shareholders can't expect much, if any, value until the business concept has been proved. Yet, that very argument is the essence of early stage investing. Yes, it is true that early stage companies are risky and that many fail. However, some are successful, and it is that "holy grail" that continues to entice entrepreneurs, angels, VCs, and others to invest in the opportunity to strike it rich.

CONCLUSION

The option-pricing method in both of its forms, Black-Scholes and lattice, is a useful tool to assist in the allocation of enterprise value among different classes of preferred and common stock, as well as warrants and options. The techniques are a little tricky at first, but with practice and the build-out of a few different models, they can easily be implemented in an early stage company valuation assignment. Of course, it will behoove you to understand the nuances of option-pricing so you can appreciate the subtleties of the math and the unique application of option-pricing to early stage company valuations.

Application of the Probability-Weighted Expected Returns Method in Allocating Enterprise Value

The probability-weighted expected returns method (PWERM), also known as the scenario method, is rooted in decision-tree analysis. In implementing the PWERM, potential future outcomes such as sale or merger, initial public offering (IPO), dissolution, or continuation as a private company are modeled and probability weighted. The PWERM is the most appropriate allocation method to use when management can reasonably predict potential future outcomes or returns are expected to include large "spikes" as value-creating events occur.

As an allocation model, the PWERM also has conceptual merit and has greater transparency than the option-pricing method (OPM), in that the consideration of the proceeds of each equity class at the date in the future those rights are expected to be exercised or abandoned is observable. Similar to the OPM, the PWERM is forward looking; it incorporates potential future economic events and outcomes into the determination of value as of the valuation date.

The PWERM, however, also has several weaknesses. This methodology can be complex and costly to implement. Whereas the OPM requires only five inputs (many of which are arguably merely "best guess" assumptions), a PWERM requires a number of assumptions about future outcomes that, realistically, are simply unknowable as of the valuation date. These assumptions are often based only on management estimates and, therefore, could potentially be biased. This potential management bias was noted by the authors of the Private Equity Valuation Guidelines when they stated, "These Guidelines acknowledge the perception that bias exists, or has the potential to exist, in a non-independent (versus independent) valuation performed by a fund's manager."[1] Nonetheless, the seasoned valuation professional should be able to ferret out egregious bias and make subjective adjustments within the PWERM to account for perceived biases, either up *or* down. More on this appears in a following section in this chapter.

Unlike the OPM, the PWERM, as used in the allocation of value for early stage companies, is not formally supported by consensus or textbook except in the AICPA Practice Aid, as far as I am aware. Analysts have been forced to construct models unique to each engagement. Because of a lack of standards and general acceptance, many alternative PWERM models have arisen, some of which can be labeled "creative" while others have to be labeled "crazy." Due to the lack of consistency among practitioners, I have observed that auditors often prefer to use an OPM because it has relatively fewer inputs, and those inputs lend themselves to auditing better than their seemingly more subjective counterparts under the PWERM. Appraisers performing a PWERM may be asked to check their allocation using an OPM during the audit review process by some audit firms with an OPM preference or policy. Some valuation firms have addressed the "OPM preference" by creating a hybrid mix of "probability-weighted expected option models," or PWEOMs. I personally think mixing and matching the OPM and the PWERM adds an unnecessary layer of complexity, but doing so seems reasonable given the uncertainties of early stage companies. This could be a good topic for an article or the next edition of this book.

Before addressing the nuts and bolts of the PWERM, I want to discuss some other thoughts about the PWERM that have come up in discussions since the AICPA Practice Aid was published in 2004. Looming large over the entire PWERM discussion is the question, does the PWERM actually provide a valuation *and* an allocation solution in one fell swoop? This question arises because in the process of implementing the PWERM, the analyst must model future possible exits for the company. In doing so, an argument is made that each discrete future exit is really a valuation of the company at some future point and that by aggregating and discounting each discrete exit, the overall value of the company can be estimated. I believe this argument has merit, so let's cover the mechanics of the PWERM in order to perform a more specific examination of this thought farther along in this chapter.

ILLUSTRATION OF THE PWERM

As discussed, the PWERM can be viewed as a method to calculate a company's enterprise value *and* to allocate that value among the different classes of equity. The steps in implementing the PWERM are generally as follows:

1. Estimate future values for each potential outcome
2. Allocate these future values to each share class
3. Discount future values to present value, by class
4. Assign probabilities to each outcome
5. Estimate share value by summing the probability-weighted outcomes

The order in which these steps should be taken has been debated in various quarters and different views have emerged. Because I'm not burdened by the facts, I can give my opinion that the steps should be taken in the order I've listed them. Why is that? In order to allocate anything, there first has to be something to allocate—hence the need to estimate future values first. The next step takes a little more thought but still follows some fairly easy logic. If the future values are discounted to present value before they are allocated, the aggregate values would necessarily change and could therefore affect the allocation of proceeds based on the breakpoint analysis that was presented in Chapter 4.

Once the future values have been appropriately allocated, Step 3 can be implemented. Because there could be numerous value outcomes that affect both preferred and common stock with different risk profiles, discounting them individually with a risk-adjusted discount rate before considering probabilities allows for a more accurate matching of risk and return. After this, the appraiser is home free, as the outcomes can be probability-weighted on a direct apples-to-apples basis. Does this make sense?

Returning to the previous illustration, the first step in applying the PWERM is to estimate the value of the company under each future scenario being considered. Here, the choices are limited, however; a company can have only one of four outcomes:

1. An IPO
2. A sale or merger
3. Staying private and continuing to operate independently
4. Going out of business

There are variations on some of these outcomes—for example, a bankruptcy under a "stay-private" outcome or an asset sale under a "sale" outcome. But for all intents and purposes, these four outcomes are the only choices a company has as it moves through its stages of development. Although these four scenarios are discussed in the AICPA Practice Aid, many practitioners think that "staying private" is irrelevant. The argument is that there is no liquidity under this scenario. Second, the stay-private scenario is typically allocated using the current method, with the allocation based on the current value rather than the future value, making this a hybrid current value/PWERM method.

Finally, there is no such thing as a successful stay-private investment for a VC firm, because it will need liquidity at some point. If the company is not successful enough for liquidity, the argument is that the stay-private scenario is really a go-out-of-business scenario. Although these are all good arguments, the stay-private scenario can be modeled by forecasting out to some point where the company is able to redeem the preferred shares and then make "constructive" dividend distributions to the common shareholders. Not pretty, but doable with a large enough budget and some creative forecasting.

Depending on the level of visibility management has regarding future exit scenarios, all four outcomes can be used, or as few as two. In general, all four are usually considered. When all four are not used, management usually says something like, "Either we're going to get sold or we're going out of business." With a comment like that, of course, the selection of "sale" and "going-out-of-business" outcomes is made easy. In practice, the earlier a company is in its development, the more difficult it is to ascertain future outcomes. In my experience, almost every early stage company has aspirations of going public; hence, most PWERMs performed at the earlier stages include an IPO outcome. At the same time, realism has become much more pervasive since the tech wreck, so it has been easy to include a "going-out-of-business" scenario at the same time. Some would say this dichotomy is contradictory, but this is the early stage realm where uncertainty is the rule rather than the exception.

When I opt to use the PWERM, I encourage my clients to consider as many outcomes as is reasonable. As a company moves into later development stages, the PWERM becomes more refined as uncertainty related to future outcomes is reduced. It follows, then, that the more outcomes that are incorporated into the PWERM, the more risk is captured in the scenarios versus the discount rates. In using the PWERM, the weighting of scenarios theoretically captures some of the risk of achieving any given scenario. The discount rate applied to the values achieved after the PWERM is applied captures another layer of risk. When more scenarios are used, more risk is captured by them and therefore the use of a discount rate to capture risk is reduced. This is the theory behind Black-Scholes that calculates infinite numbers of scenarios. In Black-Scholes, a risk-free discount rate is used as the risk of the achieving the cash flows is minimized by the scenarios. However, the inclusion of additional scenarios requires that more assumptions be made, which runs counter to risk reduction and shifts the pressure back onto discount rate selection. And you thought this was going to be easy.

Once the potential outcomes have been selected, the analyst needs to consider the company's need for future financing and the milestones the company must pass to achieve various exit events. Another advantage of the PWERM over the OPM, especially early on in the company's development, is that it allows the transparent consideration of exits at multiple future dates as well as the specific inclusion of additional rounds of financing. This can be seen in the example presented farther on in this chapter. On this point, I am often asked, "Can't I also run the OPM with different terms?" Yes, the OPM can be run with variable terms—that is, exit dates—as well, but the singular value input doesn't allow for the flexibility of the PWERM. Therefore, in my opinion, the OPM is not as effective when detailed exits at multiple dates are utilized. For example, the company may, because of its low enterprise value, enter into a transaction sooner if the product isn't expected to develop fully enough for more favorable future exit values.

Assuming that the future values have been locked in for each outcome (more on this later), the next step is to allocate these future values between each class of equity at each future event. Dates and types of future events must be considered as well as the rights and preferences of each class. For example, as noted previously, preferred stock typically has an auto-conversion feature that is triggered by an IPO. If an IPO scenario is included as one possibility, the final value conclusion will be distributed pro rata to all the common stock, assuming full conversion of all then-existing and additional required preferred stock. Consequently, the type of potential exit event could materially impact the future allocation of value.

Once allocated to the appropriate classes of stock, each future value is then discounted to the valuation date using an appropriate risk-adjusted discount rate. Another frequently discussed issue is whether to use different discount rates for the different scenarios. Some argue that the risk of the different scenarios is captured in the assigned probabilities, while others believe each outcome should stand on its own and be "risked" accordingly. In fact, the PWERM addresses risk in four ways: (1) the number of scenarios used, (2) the variability of the exit value, (3) the discount rates assigned to each scenario, and (4) the assigned probabilities.

In contrast, the OPM theoretically models infinite scenarios, so it would be appropriate to use a risk-free discount rate when using that methodology, since probabilities are assigned assuming a lognormal distribution. The

PWERM, in its basic form, models only a few selected scenarios and therefore seldom captures all the risk through probability weighting alone. This shortcoming can be addressed through the use of Monte Carlo simulations, but their use is rare in practice. Because it is typical to model only a few potential outcomes, it is common for valuation professionals to apply a higher discount rate for an IPO or an M&A scenario than for a dissolution or a stay-private scenario. While each scenario assumes a particular path and therefore would not be more risky, the variability of the exit value is likely higher with the IPO than with the M&A and dissolution scenarios. From the common stock perspective, the dissolution scenarios typically equate common stock values to zero. There is no dispersion of zero values. As a result, the variability of that cash flow is lower. Probabilities are assigned to each potential future outcome based on the facts and circumstances of each company as of the valuation date.

In order to determine appropriate probabilities for each scenario, I discuss the likelihood of each outcome with management, review any reports prepared for the company by investment banks, and research market conditions for the industry, in addition to relying on my own experience related to early stage companies. There are a few empirical studies of venture-backed company exits[2] and I have also done an updated analysis of these statistics (see Chapter 6). Again, consider the need for additional financing and the need to achieve certain milestones when assigning probabilities. Based on the probabilities estimated for the possible events, a probability-weighted value can be determined for each shareholder class.

PWERM CRITICAL ASSUMPTIONS

Critical assumptions required to perform the PWERM include:

- *Valuations.* The expected valuation under each future event outcome is estimated based on the cost, income, or market approach or a combination thereof, using management's financial projections and available market pricing data.
- *Timing.* The expected date of each exit event or outcome is estimated based on discussions with the company's management, an analysis of market conditions, and empirical data supporting the selected time periods. For example, what is the current time-to-IPO for a venture-backed company? Since this changes over time (see Exhibit 3.10 in Chapter 3), it is important to consider whether management's estimate is realistic and, if not, what is the rationale for staying with that particular

estimate. Of course, individual companies have individual time lines, but overall, the state of IPO activity will impact even the best-positioned companies.

- *Discount rates.* Risk-adjusted rates of return are selected for each scenario.
- *Discounts.* Appropriate minority or marketability discounts, if any, required to estimate the common share value under each scenario are determined.[3]
- *Event probabilities.* Probabilities should be estimated based on discussions with the company's management, an analysis of market conditions, and additional empirical support, if available.

PWERM Example

Medivice, Inc. was formed in 2001 to develop medical devices. As of the valuation date, Medivice had revenue of approximately $15 million but had not yet become cash flow positive. The company received FDA approval of one of its devices in 2007 and focused on the continuing development of its technology and on achieving broader market acceptance. At the valuation date, management projected that Medivice would require additional financing in approximately one year.

The company is authorized to issue 80 million shares of stock, consisting of 45 million shares of common stock and 35 million shares of preferred stock. The preferred stock is further divided into three million shares of Series A, eight million shares of Series B, 14 million shares of Series C, and 10 million shares of Series D. Medivice's preferred capital structure as of the valuation date is as follows:

	Issue Date	Issue Price per Share	Shares Issued	Issue Price × Shares
Series A	March 2001	$1.10	3,000,000	$ 3,300,000
Series B	January 2003	$1.40	8,000,000	11,200,000
Series C	April 2005	$1.75	14,000,000	24,500,000
Series D	February 2007	$2.65	10,000,000	26,500,000
Total			35,000,000	$65,500,000

Medivice's common stock, common stock options granted, and its yet-to-be granted option pool as of the valuation date are as follows:

Common stock outstanding at the valuation date	3,268,200
Common stock options granted as of the valuation date[4]	4,500,000
Common stock options yet to be granted as of the valuation date	3,895,250

As of the valuation date, there were 46,663,450 fully diluted shares issued or anticipated to be issued, based on the information provided here. Since management indicated that it intends to issue the entire option pool prior to a liquidity event, I have included those shares, as well as expected proceeds, into my assessment of fully diluted shares. This is a common practice among early stage companies and their investors when determining fully diluted shares for term sheets.

OVERVIEW OF STOCK RIGHTS

Chapter 2 discusses the various attributes of preferred and common stock on a theoretical basis. However, when the allocation process is initiated, a complete and thorough understanding of each right that impacts the value of other securities must be obtained so that each class of security is accorded its rightful share and in the proper order. During my long experience and exposure to the early stage realm, I have noticed that preferred stock provisions ebb and flow along with the economy. When money is plentiful and potential deals are scarce, preferred stock provisions tend to become more "common friendly." Of course, the opposite is true when money is tight and deals plentiful. At times, the provisions of previously issued preferred stock change between rounds as the economy moves up or down. Make sure the most up-to-date term sheets and articles of incorporation are obtained so the then-current operating provisions can be referenced in the allocation. Now, let's look at the provisions of Medivice's preferred and common stock.

Preferred Stock

- *Liquidation preference.* The liquidation preferences of each series of Medivice's preferred stock are as follows: $1.10 per share for the Series A, $1.40 per share for the Series B, $1.75 per share for the Series C, and $2.65 per share for the Series D. All of the foregoing preferences have been adjusted for stock splits, stock dividends, reclassifications, and similar changes, along with any declared but unpaid dividends. The Series C and D preferred shares receive their liquidation preferences on a *pari passu* basis prior to the payment of the Series A and B liquidation preferences. After payment of the Series C and D liquidation preferences, the Series A and B shares receive their liquidation payments on a *pari passu* basis prior to any payments to the common stock. After all of the preferred liquidation preferences have been met, the remaining assets are to be distributed ratably among the common stockholders. The preferred stock does not participate until conversion to common stock.

- *Dividends.* Holders of preferred stock are entitled to receive noncumulative dividends at the annual rate of 8.0 percent of the original purchase price when, and if, declared by the board. At the valuation date, no dividends had been declared on any preferred stock and none were anticipated. It would be unusual for an early stage company to declare dividends and pay those dividends in cash, given that cash is like water in the desert for early stage companies. However, I have seen instances when dividends are declared but the payment has always been in stock, the "sand" in the desert, if you will. At any rate, it is not common for early stage companies to declare dividends, so the difficulty posed by that action is not something that the analyst typically has to deal with.

- *Hierarchy.* Series C and D preferred stock are superior to Series A and B and to common stock with respect to liquidation rights. Series A and B preferred stock are superior to common stock with respect to liquidation rights. All preferred shares are superior to common stock with respect to dividend rights.

- *Conversion ratio.* All preferred shares are convertible into common stock at the initial rate of one share of common for each share of preferred. This ratio is subject to adjustment following certain dilutive events. As of the valuation date, no adjustments had been made to the conversion ratio and none were anticipated.

- *Voting.* Preferred stock shall vote together with the common stock as a single class on an as-if-converted basis.

- *Automatic conversion.* The preferred shares automatically convert into shares of common stock at their respective conversion ratios following the closing of a firmly underwritten public offering of shares of common stock of the company at a price per share not less than $4.00 per share, for a total offering of not less than $30 million. The preferred stock shall also automatically convert into common stock at the election of the holders of at least two-thirds of the outstanding shares of all preferred shares.

- *Redemption.* Holders of preferred stock have no right to force redemption.

Common Stock

The common stock has one vote per share and is subordinate to preferred stock in terms of liquidation, distribution of assets, and dividends.

IDENTIFICATION OF OUTCOMES

Based on discussions with management, there were three potential future outcomes for Medivice as of the valuation date—dissolution, sale, or an IPO. Management did not believe that the company was likely to operate as a private entity in the long term due to the investors' desire to achieve liquidity. With the potential outcomes identified, the five steps of the PWERM can now be implemented as described in the following paragraphs.

1. Estimate Future Values for Each Potential Outcome

Dissolution Scenario   The company's future value under the dissolution scenario was estimated using the cost approach based on management's projections of *cash burn*. Management provided forecast balance sheets for the next 12 months, the time frame in which management would know whether a sale would be achievable or new financing could be found. Since the company would require financing in approximately one year, it was estimated that the time to dissolution was six months. According to the cash burn projections, the company would have $2.8 million in net tangible assets at this time. Although the intangible assets are expected to have tremendous value if the company can be sold turnkey or taken public, without a sale or additional financing, management didn't believe they could realize any value from the company's intellectual property. Accordingly, the net proceeds from a dissolution scenario were estimated at $2.8 million.

Sale Scenario   The potential proceeds under a sale scenario were estimated using the market approach. This scenario was assumed to occur in one year, given that the company was not able to achieve financing that would allow it to continue operating and achieve an IPO.

In implementing the market approach, an analysis of companies that had been acquired during the past three years was performed. We focused on companies that produced medical devices similar to those produced by Medivice and that were similar in their stage of development. Based on this analysis, an enterprise value to trailing 12 month (TTM) revenue multiple of 3.5 times was selected. Although revenue multiples have a bad reputation in the valuation community generally, they provide one of the few available valuation metrics for early stage companies since most, including Medivice, do not have positive cash flow. There are a number of sources for obtaining revenue multiples, but the best sources for early stage companies, if you can find them, are those that focus on early stage transactions, such as VentureOne and PitchBook.

At the time of a potential sale, management projected that Medivice would have TTM revenue of $30 million. Based on the projected revenue and market multiple data, the proceeds from a sale in one year were estimated to be $105 million. Since management did not anticipate the company would have any debt outstanding at the time of the sale, $105 million was considered both the company's enterprise value as well as its equity value.

IPO Scenario The proceeds under the IPO scenario were also estimated using the market approach. An IPO was assumed to occur in two years after the company had achieved a final Series E round of financing totaling $20 million. The Series E round was assumed to occur at the same price as the Series D and have rights and preferences equivalent to the Series C and D preferred stock. Management believed that after achieving additional financing, the company would be able to expand its sales force and increase revenue ramp, thereby allowing it to achieve an IPO.

As with the sale scenario previously described, an analysis of guideline transactions was performed. That analysis produced five companies that were considered similar enough to Medivice to derive valuation multiples. Again, due to Medivice's lack of positive cash flow, a revenue multiple was selected as most relevant. However, instead of using trailing 12 months, a cash-adjusted enterprise value-to-revenue multiple based on the next 12 months' revenue (NTM) was calculated since management expected a significant increase in revenue due to the new capital infusion. Accordingly, an NTM multiple of 4.5 times was selected. This multiple was consistent with the range assumed by investment banks in reports prepared for the company.

At the time of the IPO, management projected that the company would have NTM revenue of $70 million. Based on the projected revenue and market multiple data, the company's estimated value at IPO in two years was calculated at $315 million. The company's projected cash balance at the time of IPO was added and projected debt subtracted to determine a future equity value of $320 million under the IPO scenario.[5]

2. Allocate These Future Values to Each Share Class

To determine the value of the common stock under each scenario, it is necessary to consider the rights and preferences of the various classes of equity. For this example, the breakpoints governing the allocation of value are as follows:

	Equity Value
Series C and D receive liquidation preference	$51,000,000
Series A and B receive liquidation preference	65,500,000
Common receives value until options exercise	67,461,000
Common and options share value until option pool exercises	69,325,000
A converts to Common stock	72,358,000
B converts to Common stock	76,757,000
C converts to Common stock	84,689,000
D converts to Common stock	117,686,000

Based on these breakpoints, the common stock value under each scenario can be determined as shown in the following table. The IPO scenario includes a $20 million Series E round to which value is also allocated. Note that all classes of equity convert to common stock in the IPO scenario.

	Dissolution	Sale	IPO
Equity value	$2,800,000	$105,000,000	$320,000,000
Plus: option proceeds	—	5,972,010	5,972,010
Equity value plus proceeds	$2,800,000	$110,972,010	$325,972,010
Allocated Series A value	$—	$ 7,020,764	$ 18,039,197
Allocated Series B value	—	21,122,036	48,104,524
Allocated Series C value	1,345,098	41,863,563	84,182,918
Allocated Series D value	1,454,902	26,500,000	60,130,655
Allocated Series E value	—	—	45,381,627
Common stock	—	4,053,400	19,651,901
Common options	—	5,581,145	27,058,795
Option pool	—	4,831,101	23,422,394
Future common stock value	$—	$ 1.24	$ 6.01

3. Discount Future Values to Present Value

The future common stock values calculated in the foregoing table are discounted to present value based on the time to liquidity and an appropriate risk-adjusted discount rate. Since the focus of the appraisal is the value of the common stock, I have not considered the explicit value of the preferred stock. The present value of the preferred stock is calculated later as a "reasonableness check" of the common stock valuation and allocation. As shown, discount rates ranging from 5 percent to 30 percent have been used for the three different scenarios. These rates were estimated based on several factors, including standard cost of equity models, reference to venture capital rates of return, and my own experience in assessing risk of early stage companies. There has been a lot of discussion among practitioners about the proper selection of discount rates; ultimately, the selection will be based on the experience and assessment of the valuation professional. Since the dissolution scenario results in zero value to the common stock, the selection of a discount rate is not necessary. For the sale scenario, estimated proceeds are expected in the next year if additional financing is not obtained. A more traditional equity rate of return, 25 percent, was selected as reasonable.

Of course, a capital asset pricing model (CAPM) would most likely have been used as a base, but even then a specific company *alpha* would negate most of the theoretical benefits of the model's precision. Finally, for the IPO scenario, a relatively more subjective rate of 30 percent, as compared with the sale scenario, was selected. Venture capital firms demand significant returns for their investments. These returns can range anywhere from 25 to 75 percent or more. Exhibit 5.1 displays historical internal rates of return from 1982 through March 2009. Prior to the tech wreck in 2000, annual returns increased from 9 percent to 310 percent before falling off the cliff in 2001. Positive returns reappeared in 2004, but during the latest bear market, returns went negative again. Since Medivice was assumed to be moving toward an IPO and had made substantial progress on its business plan, a discount rate at the lower end of the range was selected. Based on these assumptions and calculations, the company's common stock would have no value if the company were dissolved, but it would be worth $0.99 per share in a sale and $3.56 if an IPO could be pulled off. Not bad, eh?

	Dissolution	Sale	IPO
Time to liquidity event (years)	0.5	1.0	2.0
Discount rate		25.0%	30.0%
Common stock per share value (PV)	$ —	$0.99	$3.56

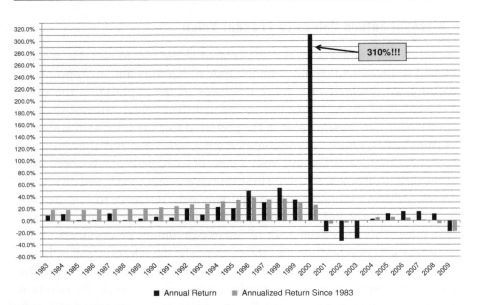

EXHIBIT 5.1 Internal Venture Rates of Return over Time and by Year

4. Assign Probabilities to Each Outcome

Now that we have placed all of the scenarios on equal footing and can compare apples to apples, the probabilities of each scenario are estimated. Probabilities were chosen for each scenario based on discussions with management and a comprehensive analysis of market conditions. In the current environment of diminished M&A activity, one has to wonder if there is a possibility of a sale at all. Nonetheless, deals do get done, even in strained economic environments. After much discussion and research, we assumed that there was a 30 percent probability that the company wouldn't make it, a 60 percent chance that it would be sold, but only a 10 percent probability that Medivice would have a successful IPO. Applying those probabilities brings us down to $0.96 per share in all ($0.60 + $0.36 = $0.96).

	Dissolution	Sale	IPO
Scenario probability	30.0%	60.0%	10.0%
Probability-weighted present value, marketable	$—	$0.60	$0.36

5. Estimate Share Value by Summing the Probability-Weighted Outcomes

Once the probability-weighted present values under each scenario have been calculated, the values can be totaled and applicable discounts can be taken. In this example, different discounts for lack of marketability were determined for each scenario. The per-share common stock values were discounted prior to being added together. The analyst may also use a blended discount for lack of marketability and apply this after the values have been aggregated.

	Dissolution	Sale	IPO
Discount for lack of marketability	0.0%	10.0%	30.0%
Probability-weighted present value, non-marketable	$—	$0.54	$0.25
Common stock fair value per share, non-marketable	$0.79		

Issues to Consider

Reasonableness Checks   When using the PWERM to value common stock, the value of the preferred stock is also determined. This can provide a useful reasonableness check of the probabilities and discount rates selected. In the example, the pre-discount values of the preferred stock would be determined as follows:

	Per-Share Value[6]
Series A preferred stock	$1.48
Series B preferred stock	$1.62
Series C preferred stock	$1.82
Series D preferred stock	$1.67

The prices determined for the preferred stock may be compared with their original issue prices to determine the effective return on the preferred shareholders' investment. If the value determined for the preferred stock is not reasonable based on the appraiser's knowledge of the company, the assumptions will need to be adjusted.

Be careful that assumptions made under the PWERM are consistent with the company's analyses under FAS 141R, 142, 123R and other fair value–based procedures.

UPDATING PWERM ANALYSES

Valuations performed for IRC 409A purposes are required to be updated at least annually. One challenge of using the PWERM lies in monitoring each assumption and documenting the changes in each assumption between valuation updates. In my experience, reviewers pay particular attention to the changes in market multiples, projections, and timing assumptions between updates.

Stay-Private Scenarios

A fourth possible scenario, not addressed in the example, is the possibility that the company does not have an exit event. Venture-backed companies typically do not intend to remain private, but it is a possible outcome for certain companies. In the case of a stay-private scenario, it is important to consider the ability of the common stockholders to realize liquidity. Due to the typical common shareholder's inability to influence the company's dividend policy or easily transfer their shares, discounts for lack of control and marketability will probably be an integral component in any valuation using a stay-private scenario.

Discounts and Premiums

Discounts for lack of control (DLOC) and lack of marketability (DLOM) will vary depending on the type of outcome expected for the company. If the expected path is an IPO or M&A transaction, the inclusion of DLOCs and DLOMs may have to be considered differently than in a stay-private scenario. However, a common stockholder will likely be subject to lock-up periods and reduced marketability in an IPO scenario as well.

A DLOC is typically approach specific. For example, a DLOC may be applied under a sale scenario, since the implied level of value is control. Because the PWERM is based on proceeds, however, some practitioners argue that a control shareholder would receive the same proceeds as a minority shareholder. Other practitioners argue that even though the ultimate proceeds implied under a sale scenario *may* be the same, the particular event is still months or years away and a true control shareholder could alter the company's course before a sale is consummated, leaving the minority common shareholder without liquidity. Thus, a DLOC would, in fact, be warranted. As usual, the application of a DLOC is fact and company specific.

As in any valuation, when applying a discount for lack of control or marketability, consider the methodology under which the equity value was determined, the company's stage of development and time to liquidity, the likelihood of future financing, and the rights and preferences of a given class of equity. Discounts, covered in more detail in Chapter 6, are ultimately based on the appraiser's judgment. If I feel I have accurately captured the liquidity risk of the equity through probabilities and scenarios, I may choose not to apply a DLOM in a PWERM.

Valuation analysts must be careful when addressing discounts and premiums, as they are often serving two masters—the IRS or the SEC and auditors. Make sure the master you are attempting to serve is well disposed toward your assumptions and selections.

CONCLUSION

Chapter 4 discussed the option-pricing method for allocating a company's enterprise value among its various classes of equity. In this chapter, an alternative allocation model was discussed, the probability-weighted expected returns method (PWERM). It was pointed out that the PWERM can be used simultaneously for valuing a company's equity securities as well as allocating that value among the various security classes. Although they are perceived by some practitioners as more subjective than the option-pricing model, a proper application of the procedures described in this chapter should result in well-supported alternative valuation and allocation methodology. Again, knowing the PWERM's limitations and benefits can provide the equipped analyst with another valuation map for navigating the uncertain waters of early stage company valuation.

CHAPTER 6

Applicable Discounts
for Early Stage
Companies

I'm always amazed at how much time and effort is expended by valuation professionals arguing about discount rates for their discounted cash flows (DCFs), volatility and other inputs for their option-pricing models (OPMs), and probabilities in the scenario approach in their valuations of early stage companies. Yet when all is said and done, the application of discounts to the aggregate values determined under whatever valuation approach was utilized may surge upward to 70 or 80 percent off the aggregate common equity value. The picture that comes to mind is a group of neurosurgeons performing an intricate procedure only to have an orderly walk in during the operation and wash everything down with a fire hose. Well, maybe it isn't that bad, but the "blunt instrument" application of discounts typically eliminates a significant portion of common equity value at the minority, non-marketable level.

Think about it: If a sensitivity analysis is performed on a selected discount rate or volatility percentage and the resulting valuation outputs differ by 40 percent or more, deeper analysis would be warranted to narrow, or at least refine, such a large gap. Nonetheless, large discounts of 40 percent or more are commonly applied, many times with little support other than passing reference to traditional discount studies. I'm not saying large discounts aren't warranted for early stage companies. On the contrary; I have beaten the "higher discount drum" for years, and I believe that current practices typically underestimate overall discounts. The following paragraphs provide discussion, empirical models, and common sense to the raging discount conundrum.

BASIS OF DISCOUNTS

Discounts for lack of marketability (DLOM) and discounts for lack of control (DLOC) are well accepted in many business valuation settings, especially the estate- and gift-tax arena, but they are less pervasive for financial statement reporting purposes. For IRS purposes, a court-tested framework for applying discounts to privately held stock exists, and it is continually tested and upgraded by research and court challenges. There is even an annual conference held by a major valuation organization[1] dedicated to discounts, primarily in the estate- and gift-tax arena. In contrast, DLOMs and DLOCs in financial accounting valuations, at least to date, lack court precedent or general agreement among practitioners.

A 2004 speech by Todd E. Hardiman, then associate chief accountant at the Securities and Exchange Commission (SEC), provides an example of this. His comments are often cited during reviews of financial reporting valuations for requiring that discounts be based on quantitative models. The issue addressed in Mr. Hardiman's speech was whether "management could demonstrate that the cash flows used in the income approach included disproportionate returns to certain shareholders. That is, could management support with *objective and reliable information* that the controlling shareholders received greater returns than the minority shareholders not through their rights as stockholders, but through their participation, perhaps as employees, in the ongoing operations of the business."[2]

This is not a new concept; adjusted cash flows can determine the level of value. The key factor for the SEC is whether there is "a disproportionate return to certain shareholders, either through the enterprise value cash flows or the equity rights." If minority and control shareholders are aligned, it is difficult to establish disproportionate returns in support of a discount between the two securities. This is a worthwhile question, but the thought process is often lost in the quest for a model or some empirical data to support a selected discount. The allocation models discussed elsewhere in this book address various rights differences between preferred and common stock, depending on the agreement. These models do not, however, capture situations in which interests are not necessarily aligned—controlling preferred as against noncontrolling common. Nor do I believe that the unique risks related to early stage companies are fully captured by traditional discount analyses or pure mathematical models. One might ask, what risks are unique to early stage companies that are not typically present in more traditional and stable businesses? Let's do a little comparison and see what we can come up with in regard to these unique risks.

As discussed in Chapters 1 and 3, early stage companies have some unique characteristics:

- New, often innovative products or services
- Large potential market for products or services
- Unproven business plan and management team
- Months or years to first revenue or profit
- Potential for rapid growth
- Securing adequate capital critical to success
- Are venture-backed and have a defined time to liquidity

In contrast, more traditional and stable companies have known products and services, have fairly defined markets and business plans, have cash flows, and have no defined time line for a liquidity event. Thus, all other things being equal, an early stage company is clearly riskier than an established business. Still, I often see the same discount analysis used for a stable business applied to an early stage company. Some practitioners argue that all of these differences in risk are captured by the valuation and allocation process so that by the time discounts are applied to the final common stock value, there is no difference between an early stage company and a stable company. However, I don't believe quantitative models can ever fully address the qualitative and subjective nuances possessed by most early stage companies. Let's take the last two points in the foregoing short list—securing adequate capital and having a defined time to liquidity.

Early stage companies, by definition, need external capital to survive. I used to joke that the CEO title for a start-up should be changed to CLC—constantly looking for cash. "Hi, I'm the CLC of Acme Start-up and I need more cash." If you have never been involved in raising capital for a start-up, you are missing out on a unique experience. All moms can relate to this because raising capital is much like childbirth: It can be extremely painful during the process but quite rewarding when it's over, assuming success, of course. But the point here is that early stage companies face "funding" risk that companies with cash flows do not. Is funding risk captured in the valuation models set forth in preceding chapters? Maybe, but perhaps maybe not. It depends on the methodology.

For example, if a scenario approach is used and the probability of achieving additional funding is specifically addressed, I might agree that it has been appropriately captured. However, in an option model, one can only surmise that the lognormal distributive nature of the returns somehow captures the risk related to the next funding or future ones. While on the topic of fundings and digression, I want to share an obsession that continues to haunt me to this day: How many companies, in total, seek funding but are ultimately unsuccessful? I believe the answer to this can have some direct impact on the application of discounts to very early stage companies, so permit me to quantify my obsession.

Since to my knowledge no comprehensive study has been made on the issue of total funding failures, I can take some liberties in interpreting the data that is available. In 2007, the National Venture Capital Association (NVCA) estimated that there were 741 venture capital firms operating in the United States with an estimated 8,900 professionals. Since VCs exist to invest, they must look at a large number of business plans to find one or two that fit their investment criteria. With this premise, let's assume that each VC professional looked at only one deal a week, a most conservative estimate. That means there were at least 462,800 "deals" looked at in 2007. The NVCA also reported that only 1,279 companies received an initial round of financing during 2007. Assuming my assumptions are reasonable, then only 0.28 percent of all companies seeking financing in 2007 were successful. That is a very small number of successful financings. Where is that risk captured? And the pattern holds pretty well over time. Even during the debauched years of the Internet heyday, only a little more than 1 percent of *all* companies seeking venture funding were successful.

I was, however, able to locate a Web site that tracks early stage submissions to its site—Angelsoft.net. During the past 12 months, Angelsoft had 22,215 deals submitted to its Web site. Of those 22,215, 1,373 (6.2 percent) made it past the first screening. Of those lucky 1,373, only 983 were invited by a VC or VCs to present their business plans. Finally, of those presenting, 467 (2.1 percent) were funded. Thus, my obsession wasn't too far off.

I don't have a definitive methodology to capture this phenomenon, but I strongly recommend that it be considered. Later in the chapter, it will be considered through an analysis of potential liquidity events. But for now, let's return to our VCs and term sheets.

Running counter to the funding risk faced by start-up companies is a characteristic of all venture funds; they must eventually liquidate and pay off their limited partners. A typical fund's tenure is five to seven years, but some may extend to 10 to 12 years before complete liquidation occurs, although such lengths are not the norm. Exhibit 6.1 demonstrates that the median time for a venture-backed company to arrive at an IPO fluctuates fairly narrowly around five to seven years, in some cases a little more

110

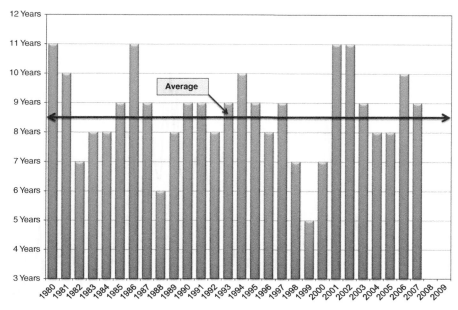

EXHIBIT 6.1   Mean Age at Time of IPO

and in some a little less. What the exhibit suggests to me and what I have observed in my involvement over the years with early stage companies is that venture funds attempt to winnow their weaker portfolios as soon as they can and pour their resources into their portfolio companies that have a higher perceived probability of success.

As shown in Exhibit 6.2, during the past 30 years there has never been any more than 275 venture-backed IPOs in any given year, and the average from 1980 to 2008 was only about 113 per year. Given the estimated

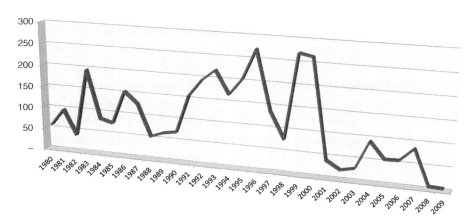

EXHIBIT 6.2   Venture-Backed IPOs

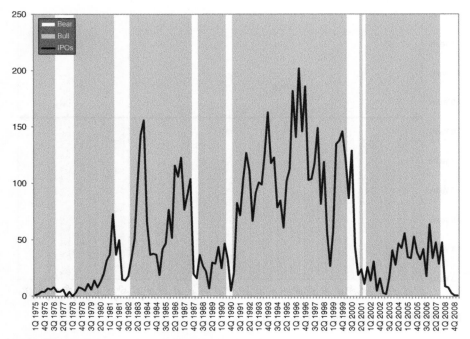

EXHIBIT 6.3 IPO Activity Contrasted with Economic Activity

number of companies seeking funding every year, the chances of making it all the way to an IPO with funding along the way are miniscule. This is especially true when the IPO window is shut or at risk of shutting (e.g., during a recession), as shown in Exhibit 6.3. This qualitative data suggests, and I believe supports, DLOMs at the higher end of the range, given that the likelihood of liquidity for early stage companies is comparatively less than for a traditional operating company, where typical DLOMs based on restricted stock or pre-IPO studies might be more applicable.

As with DLOCs in general, it is difficult to objectively support such discounts for early stage companies. Usually, cash flows inuring to both preferred and common stockholders before the liquidity event are often the same (i.e., zero); at a liquidity event, all common stock equivalent holders often receive the same dollar amount per share. In a PWERM analysis, discounts can be applied, as appropriate, to each path (e.g., discount the stay-private path but not the IPO path), but when a Black-Scholes OPM is used, it is more problematic to explain why a discount is needed and to support its quantification. A typical argument is made that since the preferred stock is usually acquired under minority, non-marketable circumstances, it is inappropriate to apply a discount to the minority, non-marketable common stock. I disagree with this assumption (except in most unusual circumstances) based on the superior rights and control positions usually held by even minority preferred stockholders. Many of these superior rights have been covered in other sections of this book.

Some valuation professionals apply lack-of-control discounts to the valuation-date enterprise value before placing the enterprise value into an option model. I believe this is incorrect. Both the OPM and PWERM are enterprise allocation models that project enterprise value into the future and then allocate that value among various classes of equity. If the enterprise value is discounted before it is grown into the future, the result may be a materially lower exit value than if the value had not been discounted before it was input into the model. When the discounted enterprise value is then allocated to the preferred and common stock, the preferred stock will be allocated an incorrectly large percentage of the total value, since the entire enterprise value was discounted, not just the common stock portion.

Quantitative measures are unreliable if the big-picture qualitative issues are not considered. Furthermore, quantitative models can be subject to a phenomenon generally known as "garbage in, garbage out." Some fact patterns cannot be modeled that easily and must therefore be tested for reasonableness using other means. The bottom line is that when a subjective judgment has a material impact on the result, objective quantitative and qualitative factors should be considered to establish why another subjective judgment would not be more appropriate.

The Section 409A guidance from the IRS requires reasonable valuation methods. A reasonable valuation method includes the consideration of asset-, income-, and market-based approaches along with "other relevant factors such as control premiums or discounts for lack of marketability."[3] I am not aware of, nor have I seen, any IRS emphasis on quantitative methods, contrary to my experience with the SEC. Mr. Hardiman outlined the SEC's view, and it appears to have found home in many accounting firm reviews. For financial reporting purposes, I have observed that quantitative analysis includes the use of put options, put-call collars, and regression analyses of restricted stock studies.

Put options have been used in support of a DLOM for some time. A put calculates a DLOM as the cost of locking in the current price to protect the downside risk of price movements during an illiquid period. The appeal of this calculation is that the formula itself and the key inputs such as the risk-free rate and volatility can be audited more easily than more subjective DLOM analyses. The term of the model is more subjective, but it has likely been vetted already through the equity allocation model. In addition, this

EXHIBIT 6.4   Black-Scholes (Outside of the OPM)

Stock Price	Strike Price	Maturity	Volatility	Risk-Free Rate (RFR)	Put Value
$4.47	$4.47	2.0 years	50.0%	5.0%	$0.98

model addresses SEC comments that the duration of the restrictions and the volatility of the underlying stock are basic factors to consider.

The put model is generally run as one data point among a number of others to consider. The problems to be aware of when relying on put-model conclusions include all of the normal caveats against using a short-term, theoretical pricing model designed for liquid securities and applying that to an illiquid security such as common stock of an early stage company. Additionally, the put option protects only against the downside price movements, which is a theoretical shortcoming of this calculation. Since for most closely held securities, a put option cannot be purchased or constructed, this quantitative model results in a minimum lack of marketability discount. Exhibit 6.4 provides an example of a protective put model used to determine implied lack of marketability. As shown, the inputs are taken from an analysis of the subject company's valuation metrics.

A synthetic collar can be created also to lock in the price by selling away the upside while protecting against the downward movements in price. To execute a collar, buy a put option and sell a call option. Like the put model, the put-collar model also results in a minimum lack of marketability discount.

SUGGESTED "CORRECTIONS" TO THE CURRENT USE OF PUT MODELS FOR QUANTIFYING DLOMS

At-the-money protective puts, similar to those shown in Exhibit 6.4, are often used to quantify discounts for lack of marketability applicable to early stage companies. There are a number of valid criticisms attacking the use of protective puts as a proxy for estimating marketability discounts. These criticisms include the fact, noted previously, that protective puts are most applicable to liquid securities, rather than to the closely held illiquid securities, typical of early stage companies. In addition, the volatility inputs used for the majority of protective puts I've seen in practice are based on the equity volatility of public companies that are much further along in their development and rarely possess the complex capital structures prevalent in early stage companies.

To address these criticisms, some superior put models that still rely on option theory have been developed; they can be modified and used in the quest for a more relevant DLOM for early stage companies. The two primary models that I have found most useful in my early stage company work are the "lookback" put option[4] by Francis A. Longstaff and the average strike Asian option[5] by John D. Finnerty. Professor Finnerty recently corrected an error in his put model that had been in use for a number of years. Be sure to utilize the corrected model. Despite their theoretical shortcomings, protective puts still remain widely popular among practitioners because of their ease of use and computation.

In most cases, the at-the-money put options are easily priced with the Black-Scholes formula. However, if we are trying to estimate the price for an at-the-money put on the common stock in the OPM framework, the correct value of the put should be determined within the option pricing allocation model as opposed to outside of it with the Black-Scholes formula. As discussed in the previous section, the reason for this is that the common equity volatility will be non-constant and the Black-Scholes formula cannot be applied in such cases.

To explore this concept, a simple example can be used. Assuming a common stock value of $4.47 per share, we need to calculate the price of an at-the-money put option (strike of $4.47) written on the common stock.

To price the put correctly within the option pricing method, an exercise breakpoint is needed for the put option, using a combination of long and short puts on the firm's asset value. However, a more familiar and straightforward method would be to price an at-the-money call option (with the same strike of $4.47) within the OPM and then find the implied value of the put option using the put–call parity relationship.

As shown, the capitalization table in Exhibit 6.5 is adjusted to include the issuance of a single at-the-money call with a strike of $4.47. The corresponding breakpoints in the option-pricing method are also modified to capture the claim of the option holder on the assets. The pre-money asset value of $50,000,000 is increased by the amount of the proceeds from the issuance of the at-the-money call ($2.48), resulting in a post-money asset value of $50,000,002.48 (the relationship is iterative because the amount of the proceeds is determined by establishing the fair price of the ATM call through the option-pricing method). The resulting allocation tables are shown in Exhibits 6.6 and 6.7.

EXHIBIT 6.5 Capitalization Table

Equity Class	Number of Shares	Liquidation per Share	Total Liquidation Preference
Series A Preferred	1,000,000	$35.00	$35,000,000
Common	4,000,000		
Options, Strike $5.00	2,000,000		
ATM Call, Strike $4.47	1		
Total	7,000,001		$35,000,000

The procedure in Exhibit 6.7 demonstrates that the fair price of an incremental at-the-money call option issued by the company is $2.48. The value of a corresponding at-the-money put option can be found using the put–call parity relationship:

$$call(S,K,T) + Ke^{-rT} = S + put(S,K,T)$$
$$put(S,K,T) = call(S,K,T) + Ke^{-rT} - S$$
$$put(S,K,T) = \$2.48 + \$4.05 - \$4.47 = \$2.06$$

where

$S = \$4.47$ is the value of the underlying common stock.

$K = \$4.47$ is the strike price for the at-the-money call/put.

$r = \ln(1 + 5\%) = 4.9\%$ is the continuously compounded risk-free rate.

$T = 2.0$ is the time frame to maturity/exit (in years).

$Ke^{-rT} = \$4.05$ is the present value of the strike price.

EXHIBIT 6.6 Allocation Table 1 ($\sigma_A = 50.0\%$)

	Breakpoint	Description	Call Value
Call 1	$ 0	—	$50,000,000
Call 2	$ 35,000,000	Liquidation Preference	$22,537,210
Call 3	$ 52,880,000	ATM Call Exercises	$14,575,552
Call 4	$ 55,000,001	Other Options Exercise	$13,857,414
Call 5	$235,000,031	Preferred Stock Converts	$ 514,603

EXHIBIT 6.7 Allocation Table 2 ($\sigma_A = 50.0\%$)

	Call Value Difference	Common %	Preferred %	ATM Call %	Options %
Call 1–Call 2	$27,462,792	0.0%	100.0%	0.0%	0.0%
Call 2–Call 3	$ 7,961,658	100.0%	0.0%	0.0%	0.0%
Call 3–Call 4	$ 718,138	99.999975%	0.0%	0.000025%	0.0%
Call 4–Call 5	$13,342,811	66.666656%	0.0%	0.000017%	33.333328%
Call 5	$ 514,603	57.142849%	14.285712%	0.000014%	28.571424%
Total Allocated	$50,000,000	$17,869,061	$27,536,307	$2.48	$4,594,632
Shares	7,000,001	4,000,000	1,000,000	1	2,000,000
Value per Share	$ 4.47	$ 27.54	$ 2.48	$2.30	

The put-call parity equality for European options is a general relationship that is model independent and is derived using no-arbitrage principles. Even though the values of the at-the-money call and put previously presented cannot be determined directly with the Black-Scholes formula and must be estimated within the option-pricing method, the relationship is still valid and can be used to find the value of the at-the-money put once the value of the at-the-money call has been solved. In the foregoing example, the put option was correctly priced at $2.06, compared with the $0.98 that one would have obtained by applying the Black-Scholes formula directly. If the put value was used as a proxy for estimating marketability discounts, the correct price of the put yields a discount of $\frac{\$2.06}{\$4.47} = 46\%$, compared with $\frac{\$0.98}{\$4.47} = 22\%$.

It should be pointed out that even though the correct price of the at-the-money put option was obtained, practitioners still question the use of protective put options as reliable references for determining DLOMs. An alternative model that is becoming more prevalent is the average strike Asian put option discussed by Finnerty (see note 5). Finnerty provides a closed-form analytical approximation for the value of the average strike put option that can be used to estimate DLOMs. Similar to the Black-Scholes formula, the formula for the price of the Asian put option is based on the assumption that the underlying geometric diffusion process has a constant volatility. Under the OPM framework, the firm's asset value follows a geometric diffusion process with constant volatility; hence, the formula can be applied to find the overall DLOM applicable to the assets of the firm. The common and preferred equity, however, do not follow a constant-volatility price process; therefore, the formula cannot be used directly to estimate the firm's individual DLOMs. Instead, the value of an average strike put written on the common (or preferred) stock is estimated using a Monte Carlo simulation.

Longstaff has conducted regression analyses of restricted stock studies to provide a quantitative indication of the DLOM. The application and inputs of this approach are mathematical and can be audited. The key drivers of this approach are duration and volatility. One criticism is that it assumes an investor could perfectly time the market. The indicated discount from this approach generally represents an upper bound to the DLOM.

An example of how a Longstaff analysis can be used is provided in Exhibit 6.8. Like the protective put, inputs for term and holding period are derived from the subject company's valuation analysis for consistency.

In the end, the appraiser's judgment and experience are critical. The key is to consider specific qualitative factors when evaluating the results.

EXHIBIT 6.8   Maximum Discounts for Lack of Marketability (DLOM) per Longstaff

---

ASSUMPTIONS:

Holding Period	5.00 Year(s)
Subject Company Volatility	60.000%

Implied Subject Company DLOM 62.13%

$$y = 0.0122x^{0.5234}$$

RESTRICTION PERIOD	VOLATILITY MEASURED AS STANDARD DEVIATION EQUAL TO:		
	10.0%	20.0%	30.0%
1 Day(s)	0.421%	0.844%	1.268%
5 Day(s)	0.944%	1.894%	2.852%
10 Day(s)	1.337%	2.688%	4.052%
20 Day(s)	1.894%	3.817%	5.768%
30 Day(s)	2.324%	4.691%	7.100%
60 Day(s)	3.299%	6.683%	10.153%
90 Day(s)	4.052%	8.232%	12.542%
180 Day(s)	5.768%	11.793%	18.082%
365 Day(s)	8.232%	16.984%	26.276%
730 Day(s)	11.793%	24.643%	38.605%
1,825 Day(s)	19.128%	40.979%	65.772%

Source: (1) Francis Longstaff, The Journal of Finance, Vol. L, No. 5, December 1995.

Despite the shortcomings of these models, they can provide an independent perspective when subjective judgments are used for material assumptions, such as the DLOM using traditional methodologies. The models used in valuation for equity compensation purposes are not overly complex, but the application of those models depends on the appraiser's experience and judgment.

DILUTION DISCOUNT

One discount I have found unique in early stage company valuations is a "dilution discount." For most early stage companies, the ability to continue the research and development efforts to achieve technological feasibility, additional financing will be required—often a lot. The source of additional financing is generally future rounds of preferred stock, resulting in dilution to current preferred and common stockholders. To estimate the dilutive effect on the common stock price, data on the average "equity give-up" for various rounds of financing can be reviewed to determine the estimated "give-up." An analysis of this data is provided in Exhibit 3.11 in Chapter 3. From this data, the analyst can estimate the potential dilution to current shareholders and consider whether a discount applies, depending on round and funding needed.

It is often difficult to gauge the dilutive impact of future rounds because the pre- and post-money values at the time of the future are currently unknown. Going back to Chapter 1, a complete grasp of the economic environment in which the company is operating and its cash "runway" along with other factors must be assessed. I often hear a simplifying assumption for future dilution that has theoretical appeal under "traditional" applications but may fall short when applied to early stage companies. That assumption is that the present value of the company's future value is equal to its value today and, therefore, future rounds would not have any dilutive or accretive impact on the company. That is a great assumption, but one that rarely holds in the real world, due to the uncertainty that is such a constant companion of early stage companies. Regardless, if that is the only basis on which to assess future dilution, I supposed it's better than nothing. Chapter 7 provides a more robust mechanism for dealing with dilution that can provide a more empirical—and therefore auditable—approach to addressing it.

THE LIKELIHOOD OF LIQUIDITY

In considering an overall DLOM based on the foregoing discussions, I analyzed data on the likelihood of a liquidity event that would result in value to common shareholders. A more comprehensive study was performed by Sanjiv Das, Murali Jagannathan, and Atulya Sarin,[6] but that study extended only through 2000 and I wanted to see what post-bubble data would show. As shown in Exhibit 6.9, based on data from 2002 through 2006, an A-stage company had only a 23.2 percent likelihood of achieving an IPO or being acquired within five years of funding. For B round companies, the probability increases modestly to 28.3 percent. However, even for companies that have received numerous inflows of funding, the highest probability of achieving a liquidity event after five years is 46.8 percent! This indicates a range of discounts for lack of marketability and a likelihood of liquidity of

EXHIBIT 6.9   Series A–K Financing

	2002	2003	2004	2005	2006
Series A Financing					
Acquired/Merged	19%	17%	11%	6%	2%
In Bankruptcy	0%	0%	0%	0%	0%
In IPO Registration	1%	1%	0%	0%	0%
Out of Business	9%	7%	4%	1%	0%
Private and Independent	68%	72%	83%	92%	97%
Publicly Held	3%	2%	1%	0%	0%
Total Receiving Series A Financing in Year					
Likelihood of Positive Liquidity Event	23%	20%	12%	6%	2%
Series B Financing					
Acquired/Merged	24%	22%	14%	9%	4%
In Bankruptcy	0%	0%	0%	0%	0%
In IPO Registration	1%	1%	2%	1%	1%
Out of Business	10%	7%	5%	2%	1%
Private and Independent	62%	65%	77%	87%	94%
Publicly Held	3%	5%	2%	1%	1%
Total Receiving Series B Financing in Year					
Likelihood of Positive Liquidity Event	28%	28%	18%	11%	5%
Series C Financing					
Acquired/Merged	29%	28%	17%	12%	3%
In Bankruptcy	0%	0%	0%	0%	0%
In IPO Registration	1%	1%	3%	2%	3%
Out of Business	10%	11%	6%	2%	0%
Private and Independent	51%	54%	67%	79%	93%
Publicly Held	8%	5%	8%	5%	1%
Total Receiving Series C Financing in Year					
Likelihood of Positive Liquidity Event	39%	35%	27%	19%	7%

(*Continued*)

EXHIBIT 6.9 *(Continued)*

	2002	2003	2004	2005	2006
Series D Financing					
Acquired/Merged	33%	27%	23%	11%	4%
In Bankruptcy	0%	0%	0%	0%	1%
In IPO Registration	0%	2%	2%	5%	3%
Out of Business	9%	9%	6%	4%	2%
Private and Independent	48%	52%	61%	73%	87%
Publicly held	10%	10%	9%	6%	3%
Total Receiving Series D Financing in Year					
Likelihood of Positive Liquidity Event	*43%*	*39%*	*33%*	*22%*	*10%*
Series E Financing					
Acquired/Merged	34%	24%	16%	13%	8%
In Bankruptcy	0%	0%	0%	0%	0%
In IPO Registration	0%	0%	1%	1%	2%
Out of Business	8%	7%	5%	3%	0%
Private and Independent	53%	47%	60%	73%	85%
Publicly held	6%	22%	17%	10%	5%
Total Receiving Series E Financing in Year					
Likelihood of Positive Liquidity Event	*40%*	*46%*	*35%*	*25%*	*15%*
Series F–K Financing					
Acquired/Merged	30%	30%	31%	15%	5%
In Bankruptcy	0%	0%	0%	0%	0%
In IPO Registration	0%	0%	2%	2%	0%
Out of Business	11%	4%	2%	4%	0%
Private and Independent	43%	48%	53%	71%	91%
Publicly Held	17%	19%	11%	8%	5%
Total Receiving Series F–K Financing in Year					
Likelihood of Positive Liquidity Event	*47%*	*48%*	*44%*	*25%*	*9%*

Source: Venture Source.

over 70 percent for very early stage companies and as high as 60 percent for more "mature" early stage companies. This is powerful empirical support to include in conjunction with traditional discount studies in assessing an applicable DLOM that the traditional DLOM studies just don't address.

CONCLUSION

A lot has been covered in this chapter in connection with discounts. Hopefully, it has provided a framework to assess a proper level of discounting for the unique risks and holding periods that are typically faced by early stage companies but are not so prevalent for traditional companies. Many practitioners don't like the subjective nature of many of these risks, but regardless of an individual's comfort level, they exist. For this reason, I can't stress sufficiently the need for practical experience in dealing with discounts and premiums for early stage companies. When challenged by an audit review or a representative from a governmental agency, these companies will be hard-pressed to counter an analyst's own experience, backed up by the foregoing data points and observations, to successfully challenge his or her selection of a particular discount. That is not to say anyone can use whatever magnitude of discount is wanted with impunity; rather, what I'm trying to convey is that a more subjective DLOM component exists with early stage companies than with traditional companies; therefore, the analyst's own experience takes on more importance when assessing a DLOM for such companies.

CHAPTER 7

Advanced Valuation Topics for Early Stage Companies

As discussed in Chapter 3, the current value method is acceptable only in limited circumstances as a preferred value allocation method for early stage companies. The probability-weighted expected returns method (PWERM), on the other hand, is virtually always an acceptable value allocation method if it is appropriately applied. Due to the apparent subjectivity of some of the PWERM's key inputs, however, it is often considered less preferable than the option-pricing method (OPM). There are facts and circumstances of specific early stage companies that argue for the PWERM over the OPM—that is, when the relevance of the PWERM outweighs its perceived subjectivity. To properly address the choice between these two allocation methods, one should focus on situations in which the OPM is less likely to provide reliable results:

- Future financing rounds are expected to occur prior to an exit event.
- Major nonfinancial milestones have not yet been resolved.
- Significant spikes in value are possible (e.g., phase success in the biotech field).
- An IPO or sale is imminent.
- The time period to exit or liquidity is lengthy.

Some add that another flaw of the OPM is that there are many-stepped paths to liquidity that flow one from another and result in different times to liquidity (e.g., "We will try to sell in 18 months if things look tough, but if we get the big sales we are hoping for we will try to IPO in two years"). However, this aspect can be addressed by running multiple OPMs with different exit dates. At any rate, the potential situations bulleted above are addressed in the following sections.

The Black-Scholes version of the OPM is not flexible. Only one input is allowed for volatility, one for time to liquidity, and one for exercise price.

An early stage entity that expects to raise future rounds of financing is more appropriately modeled as a sequence of options, otherwise known as a compound option. Future rounds of financing usually coincide with the resolution or achievement of a significant technological or market-related milestone. In concept, the OPM can be employed, but not in its Black-Scholes rendition. I provide an analysis and an example of a compound option, but other textbooks cover compound options in much greater depth than is needed here.[1]

When uncertainty exists about the future success or failure of a particular milestone, the Black-Scholes model is limited. Black-Scholes assumes that over the life of an option the value of the underlying asset (i.e., the enterprise, equity, or a segment of an enterprise) moves incrementally up or down in a formula-driven way at various points in time, based on the asset's volatility. When a major milestone is resolved, either successfully or unsuccessfully, the value of the underlying enterprise will often change by a significant rather than an incremental amount. As outlined in the preceding discussion, the presence of such unresolved risks and anticipated spikes in value suggests the need for employing a sequential or compound option solution, such as the one described in a following section.

In addition to future financial rounds and nonfinancial milestones, even "relatively mature" early stage companies can be expected to experience a final nonincremental spike in value when an IPO or other exit event becomes imminent. Although the OPM can be modified to capture the expected exit event, it is often easier to model such events using a PWERM.

The Black-Scholes model was originally developed to value short-term, traded options with contractual maturity dates. Over long periods of time (particularly with respect to emerging enterprises in industries that are significantly impacted by technological change), certain key inputs to Black-Scholes are unstable, especially expected term and expected volatility. The uncertainty regarding expected term can be handled by the use of multiple Black-Scholes models. Volatility, however, may be expected to change over time—that is, to be nonconstant. This changing volatility, if material, cannot be addressed in a Black-Scholes model, but can be dealt with in a lattice framework.

In summary, the Black-Scholes version of the OPM may not be reliable in a variety of situations. More advanced versions of the OPM—compound options utilizing lattice models—can overcome these limitations. However, the modeling can be very complex, and the results may be difficult to audit if the valuation is being reviewed by a company's auditors. In many of these situations, the PWERM may become a preferred alternative to the OPM, unless the audit reviewers possess the sophistication to understand and grasp the complexities of lattice models.

UTILIZING THE OPM AS A "VALUATION" METHODOLOGY

The most frequently encountered application of the OPM is in its role as a value allocation method among different classes of stock—that is, in situations where the aggregate value of a company's equity has been determined by some other approach or method, such as a discounted cash flow analysis or market approach. This value then becomes the underlying value input in the OPM to facilitate the allocation of value to preferred and common stock. In these situations, the value of the common stock, once determined, becomes an input into a third valuation model, such as a Black-Scholes model, to arrive at the value of the related options. However, the OPM in its more flexible forms, including the binomial method discussed subsequently, can also be used to value the underlying asset, allocate the value to various classes of equity, and value the options, simultaneously. In essence, three valuation steps are collapsed into one modeling exercise.[2]

Although theoretically valid and conceptually superior to the "three-step" approach generally employed, compound options have two primary drawbacks:

1. They can be very complex.
2. They are more difficult to audit than a Black-Scholes model.

However, the arguments in favor of using compound options include their ability to capture all the key variables and their interactions within a single framework, thereby allowing the practitioner to capture and model the complexity of the actual business situation.

SEQUENTIAL AND COMPOUND OPTIONS

This section demonstrates more complex option-pricing models, primarily the binomial model in a variety of formulations, to address some of the perceived shortcomings of the Black-Scholes model. The primary short-comings that need to be addressed are the following:

1. The inability to address spikes in value due to the success or failure of future milestones (e.g., financing rounds and technological and market risk resolution)
2. The inability to capture certain dilutive impacts

The framework introduced in this section employs an expanded version of the OPM to serve simultaneously as both a valuation and an allocation method. The use of an expanded OPM can address situations where the subject company faces multiple future risks; these risks resolve in different ways and over different time frames. Furthermore, future financing rounds—and thus, dilution of existing equity investors—is typically contingent on the resolution of these risks; if the milestones are not met, it is unlikely the company will receive further funding, and this probability of failure should be explicitly addressed in the valuation.

As an example, a multistage binomial model is used to illustrate the valuation of the aggregate equity; the same model is then also used to allocate value among various classes of equity. First, an example is presented to illustrate how the expanded OPM model can capture expected or anticipated future dilutive events. This same example is then expanded to address the resolution of future technological risks.[3]

The hypothetical facts for our example are as follows:

- Consider a development stage company that, *but for* the need for future financing, is currently valued at $1.0 million.
- The current capital structure includes both Series A preferred and common stock.
- The annual volatility of the company's assets (including its intellectual property) is 60 percent.
- The business opportunity will require external financing of $500,000 at the end of year one (Series B) and $1,000,000 of external financing at the end of year three (Series C), when the company is expected to be sold.
- The risk-free rate is 4 percent.

Clearly, the current equity owners (Series A preferred and common stock) will be diluted (from a perspective of percent of aggregate equity owned) if these future rounds of financing are needed and secured. The PWERM can handle this dilutive impact, but it requires the use of assumptions that may be difficult to support empirically. The prevailing versions of the OPM used by most valuation practitioners cannot model this fact set as easily. Neither the PWERM nor the simple OPM are very useful in addressing a *key risk*: Will the future financing rounds be successfully secured? The simple OPM implicitly assumes, for example, that the future pre-exit Series B round will be obtained; the specific scenarios in the PWERM addressing future rounds explicitly assume that a B round will be obtained (but a scenario can also be included in which a B round fails). A successful B round is implied by the fact that all the scenarios go to the three-year exit date; no failure ever occurs at the time of the Series B round, one year from the valuation date. The extended OPM (EOPM) described subsequently, takes this risk explicitly into account. Thus, it serves first as a valuation model and, as we will see, as an allocation model.

To capture the risk of successful or unsuccessful Series B and C rounds (if unsuccessful, the opportunity expires worthless[4]), we model the business opportunity as an option that has two exercise prices at two different dates. In our initial example, the underlying business has a "but for" present value of $1.0 million, an exercise price of $500,000 at the end of year one (option 1), and a second exercise price of $1,000,000 at the end of year three (option 2).

To capture the complexity of this assumed company, the Cox-Ross-Rubinstein version of the binomial model is employed. To solve for the value of the aggregate equity, we first model the evolution of the value of the underlying opportunity that is currently worth $1.0 million. The "asset tree" for the three-year period is presented here, in thousands. We have broken this three-year period into 12 periods such that each step represents three months (see Exhibit 7.1).

Exhibit 7.1 shows the impact of the expected volatility of 60 percent on the value of the underlying opportunity. At the end of the first three-month period, the value will have moved up to $1,350,000, or down to $741,000. This process is repeated until, at the expected exit date in three years, the opportunity's value theoretically ranges from a high of $36,598,000 (12 consecutive up moves, a *very small* probability) to a low of $27,000 (12 consecutive down moves, also a *very small* probability).

All options, whether simple or complex, are solved in the same manner—future to present, or right to left. Consequently, the second option, corresponding to our hypothetical Series C round, is addressed first.

EXHIBIT 7.1 Evolution of Expected Opportunity Value

Period Value of Opportunity	0	1	2	3	4	5	6	7	8	9	10	11	12
													36,598
												27,113	
											20,086		20,086
										14,880		14,880	
									11,023		11,023		11,023
								8,166		8,166		8,166	
							6,050		6,050		6,050		6,050
						4,482		4,482		4,482		4,482	
					3,320		3,320		3,320		3,320		3,320
				2,460		2,460		2,460		2,460		2,460	
			1,822		1,822		1,822		1,822		1,822		1,822
		1,350		1,350		1,350		1,350		1,350		1,350	
	1,000		1,000		1,000		1,000		1,000		1,000		1,000
		741		741		741		741		741		741	
			549		549		549		549		549		549
				407		407		407		407		407	
					301		301		301		301		301
						223		223		223		223	
							165		165		165		165
								122		122		122	
									91		91		91
										67		67	
											50		50
												37	
													27

130

The solution in Exhibit 7.2 starts at the time of exit (end of period 12), at which time the Series C round is assumed to be successful only if the company is worth more than the required $1,000,000 investment. The financing will be obtained at any of the top six nodes in the asset tree that have values in excess of $1,000,000. The solution tree therefore has six in-the-money solutions, in which the pre-money values (total value net of the required new money of $1,000,000 at time of exit) range from $822,000 to $35.598 million. You should note that these period-12 values are net of the dilution due to the Series C round that occurs at the exit date but do include some (currently unknown) portion of the value that belongs to the Series B, Series A, and common investors. The derivation of this "unknown" portion is demonstrated in a following section.

Now that the period-12 solutions have been calculated, they are then probability weighted and discounted back one period at the risk-free rate of 4 percent (or approximately 1 percent per quarter), to arrive at period-11 values. The same process is repeated to arrive at discounted values for each preceding period. However, at period 4, corresponding to the end of the first year, the first option, option 1, must be evaluated so that any needed adjustments can be made. The company will receive a Series B round only if the value of the overall business opportunity exceeds the $500,000 strike price represented by the Series B investment. Accordingly, the year-one (period 4) values delineated in Exhibit 7.2 have been probability weighted, discounted, and then compared to the $500,000 strike price. If the value of any individual node exceeds $500,000, the Series B proceeds (i.e., $500,000) are deducted; if it is less than $500,000, the hoped-for financing is not obtained, and the business opportunity is assumed to be abandoned. These net values are now "cleansed" of the value attributable to the Series B round and are weighted and discounted back to the valuation date, producing a value of $165,830, which can then be allocated to the Series A and common stock investors.

ALLOCATING THE RESIDUAL VALUE

The residual $165,830 value obtained in the foregoing text is the appropriate value to be allocated to the Series A and common stock investors. However, before this OPM model can be used to allocate value between these two shareholder classes, the solution tree must first be cleansed of that

EXHIBIT 7.2 Value of Current Equity

Value of Current Equity	0	1	2	3	4	5	6	7	8	9	10	11	12
													35,598[A]
												26,123	19,086
											19,105	13,890	10,023
										13,909	10,043	7,176	5,050
									10,062	7,196	5,069	3,492	2,320
								7,215	5,089	3,511	2,340	1,470	822
							5,108	3,530	2,359	1,489	842	360	0
						3,556	2,391	1,532	903	455	157	0	0
					1,928[B]	1,577	961	526	237	69	0	0	0
				1,127	513	585	297	121	30	0	0	0	0
			618	225	0	163	60	13	0	0	0	0	0
		325	98	0	0	29	6	0	0	0	0	0	0
	165.83	43	0	0	0	3	0	0	0	0	0	0	0

Notes: [A] The highest year-three (period 12) outcome of $35,598,000 is calculated by taking the highest asset value of $36,598,000 in the prior calculations less the $1,000,000 "exercise price" or dilution due to the Series C investors, who are expected to invest at that time.

[B] The highest year-one (period 4) outcome of $1,928,000 is calculated as follows: 44.2 percent probability of period 5 value of $3,556,000 plus 55.8 percent probability of period 5 value of $1,577,000 = $2,452,000; this amount is discounted at the risk-free rate of 4 percent (1 percent per quarter), producing a value of approximately $2,428,000. Since this value is in the money, the $500,000 Series B round is successful. Reducing the value of the opportunity by the exercise price or dilution due to Series B investors, the net value is $1,928,000. This is the value retained by the Series A and common stockholders.

132

portion of value attributable to the future Series B investors. The process can be described as follows:

1. Determine the extent to which the Series B investors dilute the holdings of the Series A and common stock holders at the end of year one (assuming a successful Series B milestone).
2. Determine how this year-one financing affects the year-three exit values (i.e., how much of each year-three value belongs to the Series B investors).
3. Remove the Series B dilution from the exit date values (year three).

Once the foregoing steps have been completed, the year-three (period 12) values are cleansed of the both the Series B and the Series C dilution and represent only the value attributable to Series A and common stockholders. The remainder of the allocation is trivial; each year-three value is evaluated based on the rights and preferences of the Series A preferred stock as opposed to the common stock, and solved as in the simple, non-dilution case. The objective, therefore, is to develop an equivalent solution tree that produces the same valuation answer ($165,830) but with the impact of both Series B and C rounds removed. This equivalent solution is presented in Exhibit 7.3.

Before addressing the quantitative development of this adjusted solution, it is worthwhile to examine it qualitatively. We start by comparing the top three in-the-money nodes at the end of period 12, as shown in Exhibit 7.4.

Certainly, the dilution, or ownership given up, due to the final, Series C round is intuitive. The greater the value of the opportunity *at the time of the Series C round*, the less the amount of that value the existing classes (period 12 pre-money investors) need to give up for the $1,000,000 investment. At time of exit, the Series C investors will receive only 2.7 percent of the aggregate value at the highest outcome, 5.0 percent at the next-highest, and 9.1 percent at the third-highest outcome. These calculations can be easily performed once the inputs and model are understood. For example, at the highest outcome, the new investors receive $1,000,000/$36,598,000, or 2.7 percent of the value. However, another step must be taken before we can allocate the residual value to the Series A preferred and common stockholders.

These values, after being reduced for the Series C dilution, now must be adjusted again to remove the dilution, or equity give-up, to the Series B investors. Again, the results are intuitive; the higher the ending valuation,

EXHIBIT 7.3 Expansion of Current Equity

Period Expansion of Current Equity	0	1	2	3	4	5	6	7	8	9	10	11	12
	165.83	276	452	730	1,158	1,809	2,783	4,219	6,312	9,330	13,639	19,733	28,267
		82	141	241	403	663	1,070	1,695	2,637	4,035	6,084	9,057	13,326
			36	65	116	204	352	594	979	1,577	2,483	3,838	5,838
				13	26	49	91	167	300	524	887	1,454	2,323
					4	8	16	32	65	128	245	454	792
						1	1	3	7	16	37	85	193
							0	0	0	0	0	0	0
								0	0	0	0	0	0
									0	0	0	0	0
										0	0	0	0
											0	0	0
												0	0
													0

EXHIBIT 7.4 Comparison of Top Three Value Nodes

Outcome	Total Value (C, B, A, Common)	Less % to Series C	Adjusted Value (B, A, Common)	Less % to Series B	Adjusted Value (A, Common)
Highest	$36,598,000	2.7%	$35,598,000	20.6%	$28,267,000
Second	$20,086,000	5.0%	$19,086,000	30.2%	$13,326,000
Third	$11,023,000	9.1%	$10,023,000	41.8%	$ 5,838,000

the lower the "give-up" to Series B investors. This quantitative solution is developed in the following subsections.

Dilution Due to Series B Round as of the End of Year One (Period 4) The highest post-money value at the end of period 4 is $2,428,000. As discussed previously, the first solution tree shows the net value after the $500,000 investment—$1,928,000. Therefore, the implied dilution at this node is $500,000/$2,428,000, or approximately 20.6 percent, leaving the Series A and common investors with 79.4 percent of the residual value. The same calculation for the next highest post-money value at the end of period 4 produces a significantly higher dilution, 49.4 percent ($500,000/$1,013,000), leaving 50.6 percent of the residual value to the Series A and common stock investors.

Impact of Pre-Exit (Period 4) Dilution on Exit Date (Period 12) Values We have already calculated the share of the value that goes to the Series B investors at the end of period 4 and noted that it varies depending on the value of the opportunity *at that time*. Next, we need to trace each of these period-4 dilutive impacts into the respective period-12 results. Using the standard binomial distribution, we know that there are 16 outcomes at the end of period 4; the highest and lowest values can be reached in only one way—by four up and four down moves, respectively. The median outcome, on the other hand, has the highest probability because it can be reached in six ways (or along six paths). The relevant binomial distribution (also known as Pascal's triangle) is presented in Exhibit 7.5.

We also know how many paths lead to period-12 exit values—2^{12}, or 4,096 separate paths. Only one path (12 consecutive up moves) reaches the highest period-12 value. Similarly, 12 paths reach the second-highest value (11 up moves and one down move, which can happen in 12 different patterns), and so on. Therefore, we can calculate how many paths start at

EXHIBIT 7.5 Pascal's Triangle

Period	0	1	2	3	4
					1
				1	
			1		4
		1		3	
	1		2		6
		1		3	
			1		4
				1	
					1

any particular period-4 node and finish at any particular period-12 node. The easiest example is the highest period-12 value; there is only one path that reaches it, and it can be reached only by passing through the highest node at the end of period 4. Thus, the dilutive impact at this period 4 node (20.6 percent given to Series B, 79.4 percent retained by Series A preferred and common investors) is preserved at the highest period-12 node. The highest value at the exit date ($35,598,000) is thus shared as follows: 20.6 percent, or approximately $7,331,000, to Series B preferred and 79.4 percent, or $28,267,000, to the Series A preferred and common stock.

This process is repeated for each period-12 value. The next highest period-12 value, $19,086,000, can be reached along 12 different paths. Eight of these paths emanate from the highest node in period 4; one path emanates from the second-highest node in period 4, but this period-4 node itself represents four different paths. Therefore, the other four paths to the second-highest period-12 value all emanate from the second-highest period-4 node. To calculate and remove the dilutive impact on the second-highest period-12 value, therefore, we weight the dilution that emanates from the end of period 4: eight paths that had 20.6 percent dilution and four paths that implied 49.6 percent dilution, for a weighted dilution of 30.2 percent. Alternatively, we can say the Series A preferred and common stock investors retain an implied 69.8 percent share (1–.302) of the second-highest exit (period-12) value: $19,086,000 times 69.8 percent, or approximately $13,326,000. The alternative solution tree cleansed of the Series B dilution is presented in Exhibit 7.3.

As mentioned, once the solution tree is reduced to the values attributable only to valuation date investors (Series A preferred and common stock), it is "solved" in the usual right-to-left manner discussed herein. As illustrated in Exhibit 7.3, the value is identical to our previous results when both options 1 and 2 were evaluated. The valuation specialist can now easily evaluate the optimal behavior of the Series A preferred and common stock investors at each of these period-12 exit values, based on the respective rights and preferences of each class.

It is important to note the distribution of period-12 outcomes in this solution. In particular, it is clear that the initial early stage investors get the greatest benefit at the highest exit values and, more important, that their share of the value falls rapidly. This is precisely what is often observed in a more traditional "waterfall" analysis. At lower values, the more senior investors (in this case, Series B and C preferred shareholders) receive much higher portions of the exit value. Therefore, the foregoing distribution of values is consistent with expected common-sense results.

FURTHER EXTENSIONS FOR COMPOUND OPTIONS

The compound option model can be extended to solve additional valuation issues. An excellent example, one that matches many real-life situations, is to modify the assumed facts by introducing a second, nonfinancial risk. Assume that the anticipated Series B round depends not only on the value of the business opportunity (i.e., it must have a post-money value in excess of $500,000 to induce the Series B investors), but also that a key technology milestone must be achieved as of the same date. Further, assume that as of the valuation date, management believes there is only a 75 percent chance that this technology risk will be successfully resolved. The impact of this new factor is easily captured with a binomial model but is often impossible to calculate with a simple Black-Scholes model. Using the same base data, the revised solution tree incorporating this factor is presented in Exhibit 7.6.

Note that in the previous example, the highest period-4 value was $1,928,000. Under this new set of factors, however, there is only a 75 percent chance of achieving a $1,928,000 value, thereby reducing the highest period-4 value to $1,446,000. Although the dilutive impact is not affected by the 25 percent chance of technological failure in this particular example, there may be circumstances that could be impacted by probabilities of success. As is frequently the case, new (Series B or C) investors will provide funds only if the technological risk is favorably resolved. Thus, if the Series B round is successful, the dilutive impact will be

EXHIBIT 7.6 Value of Current Equity with Technology Overlay

Period Value of Current Equity

0	1	2	3	4	5	6	7	8	9	10	11	12
												35,598
											26,123	
										19,105		19,086
									13,909		13,890	
								10,062		10,043		10,023
							7,215		7,196		7,176	
						5,108		5,089		5,069		5,050
					3,556		3,530		3,511		3,492	
				1,446		2,391		2,359		2,340		2,320
			845		1,577		1,532		1,489		1,470	
		463		385		961		903		842		822
	243		169		585		526		455		360	
124.37		74		0		297		237		157		0
	32		0		163		121		69		0	
		0		0		60		30		0		0
			0		29		13		0		0	
				0		6		0		0		0
					3		0		0		0	
						0		0		0		0
							0		0		0	
								0		0		0
									0		0	
										0		0
											0	
												0

identical to our previous example. The equivalent solution tree, cleansed of the Series B dilution but incorporating this new factor, is presented in Exhibit 7.7.

VENTURE CAPITAL RATES OF RETURN

Whenever I have spoken about valuing early stage companies with valuation professionals, a discussion about venture capital rates of return is inevitable. I touched on this topic in Chapter 5, but now I want to provide a little more information on the subject. Based on data from the National Venture Capital Association, returns on venture capital investments have been all over the board, depending on the year of measurement and the length of time investments are measured. As can be expected, the bulge of the Internet bubble in the late 1990s has skewed all return measures that include that time period. For example, the single-year return to limited partners in the year 2000 was 310 percent, whereas the following year it was negative 17.6 percent (see Exhibit 5.1 in Chapter 5).

I would like to break those returns down a little more to see which investors really made the most money on their investments. As shown in Exhibit 7.8, returns for different time horizons varied considerably by stage of investment. Interestingly, over the 20-year horizon, only seed/early focused was able to break 20 percent. Some investors would consider that a whole lot of risk compared to not a whole lot of return.

The results are little different for shorter time periods measured by the vintage year (the year the fund was started), but the overall pattern, greatly influenced by the Internet bubble, remains familiar (see Exhibit 7.9).

When discussing returns, no discussion is complete without comparing VC returns to alternative investment returns. As shown in Exhibit 7.10, the hyped advantages of venture capital investing don't appear all that great. Again, the skewed Internet bubble period makes up for most of the superior returns from venture capital from 2000 to 2003 before VC returns went back to the returns reported by the S&P 500 and the Nasdaq.

Finally, as noted in the AICPA Practice Aid, two studies have been published on "required" rates of return for venture capital funds. In addition, a third publication, by William D. Bygrave, outlining venture capital rates of return is available. A summary of these studies is shown in Exhibit 7.11. Notice how Plummer and Scherlis provide very high ranges of acceptable rates of return by stage. I have queried a number of venture capitalists about their required rates of return and I get the response "It depends" more often

EXHIBIT 7.7 Solution Tree with Technology Overlay

Period Expansion of Current Equity	0	1	2	3	4	5	6	7	8	9	10	11	12
	124.37	207	339	547	869	1,357	2,087	3,164	4,734	6,998	10,230	14,799	21,200
		61	106	181	302	497	803	1,271	1,978	3,026	4,563	6,793	9,995
			27	49	87	153	264	446	735	1,183	1,863	2,879	4,379
				10	19	36	68	125	225	393	665	1,091	1,742
					3	6	12	24	49	96	184	340	594
						0	1	2	5	12	28	63	145
							0	0	0	0	0	0	0
								0	0	0	0	0	0
									0	0	0	0	0
										0	0	0	0
											0	0	0
												0	0
													0

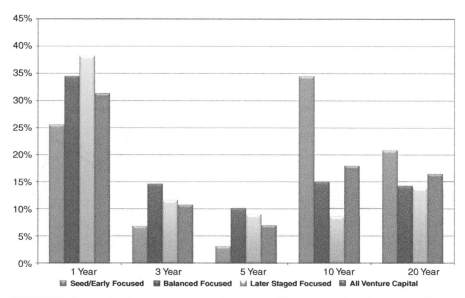

EXHIBIT 7.8   Net IRR to Investors for Investment Horizon Ending September 30, 2007, for Venture Capital Funds by Stage

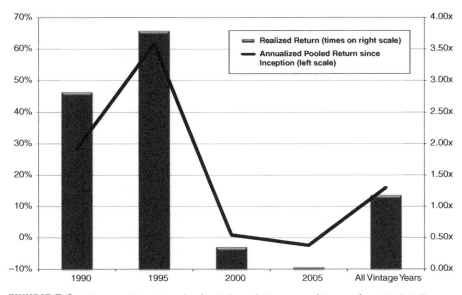

EXHIBIT 7.9   Venture Year Results for Selected Years as of September 30, 2007

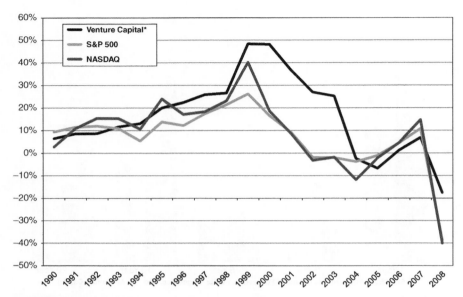

EXHIBIT 7.10   Net IRR Five-Year Rolling Average Venture Capital versus Public
Markets

than not. "From what perspective?" they ask me. When I ask about the
return requirements on their individual portfolio companies, most of their
responses are in line with those quoted in the exhibit. The reason most cite
for the very high required rates of return for start-up or first-stage companies is what I have been saying throughout this book: "Since so many
very early stage companies fail, we (the VCs) need to receive a high return
on those that are successful to make up for the losses we had on our failures." However, most VCs are not utilizing discount rates to employ in
a discounted cash flow model for early stage companies, given that most

EXHIBIT 7.11   Required Rates of Return

Stage of Development	Plummer[5]	Scherlis and Sahlman[6]	Bygrave[7]
Start-up	50%–70%	50%–70%	60%–80%
First stage or "early development"	40%–60%	40%–60%	40%
Second stage or "expansion"	35%–50%	30%–50%	30%
Bridge/IPO	25%–35%	20%–35%	25%

142

believe early stage company forecasts are really only Excel exercises. That makes sense to me!

EXECUTIVE STOCK COMPENSATION

Although not specifically related to the valuation of early stage company securities, I am constantly consulted and asked about the amount of equity that newly hired, nonfounder, C-level executives and directors typically receive upon joining a start-up company. Although there is a broad range of percentages, overall averages provide a reasonable starting point or benchmark. There are a number of compensation consulting firms that conduct studies and provide guidance on stock compensation for early stage companies, but the best source I have found is CompStudy. CompStudy publishes an annual report of equity and cash compensation that provides compensation data on 25,000 top management positions and Boards of Directors at 5,000 private companies in technology and life sciences. Data are analyzed by founder/nonfounder status, company revenue and headcount, geography, business segment, and number of financing rounds raised.

My experience matches the general averages in the CompStudy report and is summarized below by the percentage of average equity granted to a newly hired C-level executive:

- Chief Executive Officer 5.0%
- President/Chief Operating Officer 2.5%
- Chief Financial Officer 1.0%
- Chief Technology Officer 1.0%
- Vice President—Business Development 1.5%
- Outside Directors 0.25%
- Option Pool 20.00%

CONCLUSION

I have demonstrated how the OPM in its binomial form can be extended to capture the impact of anticipated future dilutive events in a rational and objective manner as well as to address nonfinancial risks such as milestone success and overall probabilities of success. The example presented herein, in which each time interval is a three-month period, was selected for ease of explanation. In an actual valuation, I suggest that an increased number of intervals per year be used to increase the accuracy and flexibility of the model. The conceptual framework of this expanded model is not affected by the number of intervals. The widely accepted strengths of the OPM—its rich set of potential outcomes, its objective risk-neutral probabilities, and its use of market-derived inputs such as volatility and risk-free rates—within this framework make it a useful alternative to the PWERM whenever future dilutive events, associated technology risks, or other unique risks are anticipated.

I also provided some data points on venture capital returns. Surprisingly, venture capital rates of return aren't all that glamorous compared with the stodgy old S&P 500 or Nasdaq unless, of course, you had the requisite wisdom, foresight, capital, and access to venture investing in the middle to late 1990s.

Finally, for the curious, I provided some observations on my experience related to the issuance of stock options to C-level executives.

Appendix A

The following article was published in the *BV Update Newsletter* in October 2007. It addresses the inclusion of in-the-money and out-of-the-money stock options in the option-allocation model as referenced in Chapter 4.

ALLOCATION OF ENTERPRISE VALUE USING THE OPTION-PRICING METHOD: TREATMENT OF DERIVATIVES ON COMMON STOCK

by Neil J. Beaton and James K. Herr

Abstract: The AICPA practice aid *Valuation of Privately-Held-Company Equity Securities Issued as Compensation* was issued in April 2004 following two years of collaborative effort by members of the Big 4 and other top accounting firms, business valuation experts, academics, and legal and venture capital practitioners. This work was supported by the AICPA, the FASB, and the SEC. Although considered comprehensive and cutting edge at publication, in hindsight, it only provides a rudimentary examination of the various allocation methods for purposes of enterprise value allocation. Based on over three years of subsequent experience and additional research, coupled with the opportunity to have reviewed numerous reports prepared by a wide variety of valuation firms from the sole practitioner to the Big 4, this article sets forth an appropriate methodology for including outstanding options and warrants on common equity when one uses the option-pricing model for allocating enterprise value[1] among different classes of stock.

With the introduction of the American Institute of Certified Public Accountants' (AICPA) practice aid *Valuation of Privately-Held-Company Equity Securities Issued as Compensation* (Practice Aid), it is generally accepted in tax compliance and financial reporting that there are three methods available for allocating a company's enterprise value among its various equity classes: current value method, probability-weighted expected returns method (PWERM), and the option-pricing method.[2] According to the Practice Aid, the current value method is generally used for companies where

(1) the going concern assumption is questionable or a liquidity event is imminent, or (2) operations are so nascent that no material progress has been made on the business plan or little to no equity value has been created. Generally these companies are early-stage, pre-revenue or have suffered a recent down round or equity cram down. As a result of these restrictions to its use, the other two equity allocation methods are more prevalent in practice.

The PWERM assigns probabilities to various possible future outcomes, such as an initial public offering (IPO), sale, steady-state, or dissolution of the firm. The enterprise value under each possible future outcome is assessed; equity allocation is performed for each scenario as if the current value method were being performed at each expected scenario liquidity date. Finally, the values under each scenario are adjusted for the time value of money back to the valuation date, and a weighted average of values under each possible future outcome is calculated based on the assigned probabilities for each outcome.

The option-pricing method is based on the theory that the value of various components of enterprise value (such as equity classes or debt) can be viewed as equivalent to various combinations of or portions of combinations of short and long call options on the enterprise value of a firm. It can be shown that the payoff to debt or simple preferred stock can be estimated using a combination of a long and short calls with different exercise prices (commonly called a "bull spread"). If we assume no debt, the payoff to simple preferred stock is a long call with an exercise price equal to a number close to zero, combined with a short call with an exercise price equal to the liquidation preference for the preferred stock.[3] If there are multiple classes of preferred stock, the long call will have an exercise price equal to the sum of all liquidation preferences with claims prior to the preferred class being valued, and a short call with an exercise price equal to the sum of all liquidation preferences with claims prior to the preferred class being valued plus all liquidation preferences with claims in the same priority class as the preferred class being valued. Common equity is then valued as a call option with an exercise price equal to the sum of all liquidation preferences.[4]

Options on Common Stock in the Option-Pricing Model

The Practice Aid provides little or no guidance on more complex capital structures frequently encountered in today's sophisticated venture capital and private equity world. Of necessity, the valuation analyst needs to remain flexible as more ingenious and ever more complex securities will continue to be created. As such, the purpose of this article is to assist in establishing current "best practices" when utilizing the option-pricing method for allocating enterprise value among capital structures that include outstanding in-the-money and out-of-the money options on common stock as of a given valuation date. Since equity is viewed as an option on the firm, options on equity can be viewed as options on options.[5] Despite this additional layer of complexity, derivatives can be easily incorporated into an option-pricing model, based on appropriate assumptions.[6]

The decision to exercise or to allow common stock options to expire unexercised is based on the per share value of the common equity on the date of an anticipated liquidity event. If the common stock option is in-the-money as of the liquidity event, the option holder would rationally choose to exercise the option. However, if the option is out-of-the-money, the option holder would rationally allow the option to expire worthless. Since options are not typically assumed by an acquiring company, these are usually the only two options available to an option holder.

The determination of the enterprise values at which option holders will exercise are based on (1) a comparison of the common equity per share value to the strike price of each common stock option grant, and (2) the amount of exercise proceeds for options with lower strike prices. Although the strike prices for the bull spreads under the option-pricing method are based on enterprise values, the points at which an option holder chooses to exercise ("option breakpoints") are based on the values of common equity per share equal to the various strike prices for outstanding common stock options. Once the option breakpoints are determined, enterprise values must then be determined for each of the option breakpoints to determine appropriate strike prices for use in the option-pricing method.

Upon a given liquidity event, if the enterprise value is sufficient to provide payouts for all liquidation preferences, then the remaining value is generally available to common equity and potentially to holders of options on common equity.[7] At the point where the common equity per share value is equal to the option holder's strike price, the option holder is indifferent between holding onto the common option and choosing to exercise. For points where the common equity per share value is greater than the option holder's strike price, the option holder would rationally choose to exercise. The various points where the common equity value per share is equal to outstanding option strike prices therefore constitute the option breakpoints for the option-pricing method.

However, the strike prices for the various slices of the enterprise value call option (see Exhibit A.1, which demonstrates four slices or payoff

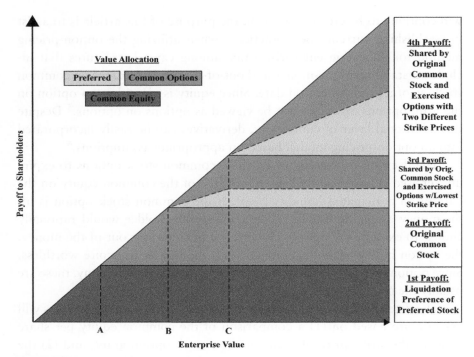

EXHIBIT A.1 Four Payoff Areas

areas) are based on enterprise value, and not on common equity per share values.

As a result, enterprise values corresponding to each option breakpoint must be determined. For the option holder(s) with the lowest strike price, the exercise proceeds will leave the common equity per share value unchanged, since there is no dilution. The extra exercise proceeds paid in for a share of stock exactly equal the price of the stock.

Since the decision to exercise is based on the common equity per share value prior to exercise, it is also the enterprise value prior to exercise that represents the strike price for the enterprise value slices. This means that for the option holder(s) with the lowest strike price, the enterprise value will be equivalent to what it would have been absent exercise. However, enterprise values at all other option breakpoints will increase on a one-to-one basis by the value of the exercise proceeds from options with lower strike prices, which will be rationally exercised. In other words, for these higher option breakpoints, the underlying enterprise values are equal to the sum of (1) all liquidation preferences, (2) outstanding shares of original common equity and options that would convert to common equity at the option breakpoint multiplied by the option breakpoint, and (3) the sum of exercise proceeds for all options that would have already exercised prior to reaching that option breakpoint. The case study provided later in this article provides an example of how this process works.

A crucial point is that an option holder would not rationally take into account his or her own exercise proceeds or enterprise value in his or her own decision to exercise. The choice is based solely on the common equity per share value prior to exercise, since actual exercise will not dilute the share price and therefore leaves the per share value unchanged.

Exhibit A.1 illustrates the impact of including options in the allocation of equity among preferred and common stock when there are common stock options with two different strike prices. The first payoff, or equity slice, goes to pay off the liquidation preferences of preferred stock until the enterprise value reaches point A. If enterprise value exceeds point A, common equity outstanding on the valuation date receives the residual value up to the point B. For enterprise values between point B and C, the common stock options with the lower strike price share the residual proceeds with the original common stock outstanding. After point C, the second set of common stock options are exercised and share in the residual value with the other group of options and the original common stock. Note that point B does not include exercise proceeds, but the enterprise value equivalent to point C includes the exercise proceeds from the exercise of the lower strike price common stock options.

The methodology we've described does not treat in-the-money and out-of-the-money common stock options as of the valuation date differently. *What is important is whether the options are considered in-the-money or out-of-the-money on the date of liquidation, which depends on any given enterprise value possible upon a liquidity event.*

Two techniques currently being used in practice for incorporating common stock options into the option-pricing model rely on a determination of the in-the-money common stock options as of the valuation date, while disregarding out-of-the-money stock options.[8] By disregarding out-of-the-money common stock options as of the valuation date, the valuation would incorrectly treat common stock options that are in-the-money as of the liquidity event. Similarly, by incorporating in-the-money common stock options as of the valuation date, the valuation would incorrectly treat common stock options that are out-of-the-money as of the liquidity event.

Another technique assumes that in-the-money common stock options as of the valuation date will be exercised as of the liquidity event, and present value the proceeds back to the valuation date, adding back the present value of exercise proceeds to the enterprise value for the purpose of determining option-pricing method values. This methodology is wrong for two reasons: (1) if in-the-money options as of the liquidity event are out-of-the-money, such treatment would overvalue the firm, and therefore overvalue the various equity classes, and (2) if out-of-the-money options as of the liquidity event are in fact in-the-money, their exercise proceeds are incorrectly excluded from enterprise value, potentially leading to an understatement of value for the various equity classes. The overall impact of using any of the three methods mentioned previously depends on the likelihood of common stock options to change their in-the-money or out-of-the-money status and the number of common stock options in the capital structure.

Case Study

The following case study provides a simple example of the methodology described previously for treatment of stock options in an option-pricing model.

Assumptions

- 100 shares of common stock
- 100 shares of Class A preferred stock, with a liquidation preference of $3 per share and convertible into common at 1:1 of face value
- 150 shares of Class B preferred stock, with a liquidation preference of $2 per share and convertible into common at 1:1 of face value
- Class A and B participate *pari passu* in liquidation up to the face value of their preferences
- 50 options on common stock with a strike price of $0.50
- Enterprise value of $1,000
- Volatility = 50%
- Three-year interest rate = 5 percent and no dividends
- Management anticipates a liquidity event in three years
- No debt

The first step under the option-pricing method is to determine the various breakpoints, including the option breakpoints.

The two preferred classes' liquidation preferences are $300 each, summing to a total of $600. Since both classes participate *pari passu*, each shares 50 percent in liquidation preferences up to $600. Thus $600 represents the first breakpoint.

The second breakpoint is an option breakpoint at $0.50, which represents an enterprise value of $650. The enterprise value at the second option breakpoint is calculated as total liquidation preferences of $600 plus 100 common equity shares times the option breakpoint, or $0.50. At a common equity per share value of $0.50, option holders would be indifferent between exercising and not exercising their options. However, at any price above $0.50 per common share, the common stock option holders would rationally exercise, since no additional value is gained by holding the option after the liquidity event.

The third breakpoint is an enterprise value of $900, which is determined by a common equity per share value of $2.00, or the point at which Class B preferred stock holders are indifferent about converting to common stock. The enterprise value is determined by adding the prior breakpoint of $650 (at an equity price of $0.50 per share) to the additional value from a common equity per share value of $2.00, which is $1.50 of additional value. This $1.50 of additional value means that the original common shares of 100 increase in value by 100 * $1.50 = $150, and that the common stock options anticipated to be exercised into common shares increase in value as well by 50 * $1.50 = $75. In addition, exercise proceeds of $25 are also anticipated as of the liquidity event, since the common equity value exceeds the strike price of $0.50 for those options. In total, enterprise value increases by $250 from $0.50 to $2.00, with $225 of the increase from capital appreciation and $25 from exercise proceeds.[9]

The fourth and final breakpoint is at $1,200, where the Class A preferred shares convert to common stock. This is the point at which the common equity per share is equal to $3.00. Again, the increase in value from the prior breakpoint of $1.00 for common equity per share is multiplied by 300, the number of common and common options already exercised and the 150 Class B preferred stock that already converted to common. Since the exercise proceeds are already included in the $900 enterprise value breakpoint, including the $25 in exercise proceeds for determining incrementally higher breakpoints would result in double counting.

Exhibit A.2 shows the long and short call option values at each of the breakpoints indicated previously. The "High Strike" row shows breakpoints discussed earlier. The "Low Strike" starts with 0 and then equals each prior breakpoint. Note that the sum of the option values equals the assumed value of the firm's equity. The allocation of value among the various equity classes is then based on each equity's participation or share of proceeds within each breakpoint band, as shown in Exhibit A.3. Exhibit A.4 shows the pro rata value of each equity slice (bull spread), based

EXHIBIT A.2   Business Enterprise Value Breakpoints

Low Strike	$ —	$ 600	$ 650	$ 900	$1,200	
High Strike	$ 600	$ 650	$ 900	$1,200	and up	Total Value
Long Call Value (Low)	$1,000	$ 559	$ 533	$ 422	$324	$ 2,838
Short Call Value (High)	$ (559)	$(533)	$(422)	$ (324)	$ —	$(1,838)
Difference (Bull Spread)	$ 441	$ 26	$ 111	$ 98	$324	$ 1,000

EXHIBIT A.3   Pro Rata Share of Each Equity Slice Payoff

				Common Equity per Share Value			
Equity Type	Class	Shares	Liq. Pref.	$0.00 $0.50	$0.50 $2.00	$2.00 $3.00	$3.00 and up
Preferred	A	100	50%				25%
Preferred	B	150	50%			50%	38%
Common		100		100%	67%	33%	25%
Options		50			33%	17%	13%
			100%	100%	100%	100%	100%

EXHIBIT A.4   Pro Rata Share of Each Equity Slice Payoff Values

				Common Equity per Share Value			
Equity Type	Class	Value by Class	Liq. Pref.	$0.00 $0.50	$0.50 $2.00	$2.00 $3.00	$3.00 and up
Preferred	A	$ 301	$220				$ 81
Preferred	B	$ 391	$220			$49	$122
Common		$ 214		$26	$ 74	$33	$ 81
Options		$ 94			$ 37	$16	$ 41
		$1,000	$441	$26	$111	$98	$324

EXHIBIT A.5   Sum of All Breakpoint Band Values

Equity Type	Class	Shares/Options Outstanding	Value by Class	Per Share/ Option Value
Preferred	A	100	$301	$3.01
Preferred	B	150	$391	$2.61
Common		100	$214	$2.14
Options		50	$ 94	$1.88

on each equity class share of proceeds among the breakpoint ranges. Finally, the sum of all breakpoint band values are taken for each equity class, and divided by the number of shares or options to determine a per share or per option value, at which point consideration of a discount for lack of marketability and/or control may be appropriate, as shown in Exhibit A.5.

Conclusion

We have expanded the option-pricing method to incorporate outstanding common stock options in performing business enterprise value allocations. Of particular importance is the differentiation between option breakpoints and enterprise value. Option breakpoints are determined based on strike prices relative to common equity per-share values. In contrast, enterprise values at an option breakpoint may include exercise proceeds, depending on the option breakpoint. The option holder's decision to exercise is based on the per-share equity value and is unaffected by the exercise proceeds from that option holder's exercise, but the exercise prices used to value the various long and short call option combinations (based on enterprise value) *are* affected by exercise proceeds.

The number of methodologies currently being used in financial reporting practice for handling common stock options in the option-pricing model is diverse. We believe this is primarily due to a lack of guidance on use of the option-pricing method for complex capital structures, but also partially due to a lack of understanding of overall option treatment. It is hoped that this article will, at the very least, begin to increase discussion regarding proper methodologies for handling complex capital structures under the option-pricing model, and at best, standardize the practice for enterprise value allocation using the option-pricing model when the capital structure includes common stock options.

Appendix B

The following article was published in *Valuation Strategies* in November 2009. It explores capital structure volatility in the option allocation model as referenced in Chapter 4.

VOLATILITY IN THE OPTION-PRICING MODEL

By Neil Beaton, Stillian Ghaidarov, and William Brigida

INTRODUCTION

This article explores and expands on the concept of volatility in the option-pricing method (OPM) as applied in the allocation of enterprise value in early stage companies with complex capital structures. The sophistication of the OPM as applied to early stage companies has increased considerably over the past five years since the AICPA's Practice Aid on the *Valuation of Privately-Held-Company Equity Securities Issued as Compensation* (Practice Aid) introduced the model to a wide audience. The Practice Aid was primarily a high-level guide in the valuation of early stage companies. Its authors recognized the limitations of that early work and encouraged readers to go beyond the rudimentary principles contained therein. There have been a number of articles published since 2004 that have endeavored to do just that. This article continues in that vein pending the publication of the updated Practice Aid that is expected in late 2009 or early 2010. In addition, this article will be expanded upon in a book that is to be published by John Wiley & Sons, Inc. in late 2009.

The specific focus of this article is to provide a review of the volatility assumption in the OPM, and to highlight several potential issues that have been observed in current practice. By considering the OPM as a straightforward extension of Robert Merton's original structural model (explained in more detail subsequently), the authors demonstrate a relationship between the asset volatility of the firm and the volatilities of the common and preferred stock. This relationship is used to gain additional insight into the proper selection of the volatility input of the OPM.

In 1974, Robert Merton published an article on the pricing of corporate debt[1] which gave rise to a class of models popularly known as "structural models." A distinguishing feature of the structural models is that they view the various securities in the firm's capital structure as contingent claims on the firm's total asset value. Merton's original set-up involved a company with a very simple capital structure consisting of a zero-coupon bond and equity. Merton realized that the equity value represents a residual claim on the firm's assets beyond the payoff of the debt principal at maturity, and as such it can be considered a European call option on the firm's assets which can be priced in the Black-Scholes option-pricing framework. He used that insight to obtain the value of the corporate debt and the associated risky interest rate for the bond.

Merton's structural model has received significant attention in academia and among practitioners, and several popular commercial applications exist, most notably Moody's KMV model which attempts to quantify the probability of default for a firm by extending Merton's framework to include various classes of corporate liabilities.[2] In the financial reporting world, one particularly common application of Merton's structural model is the "option-pricing method" which allocates the aggregate value of the firm's assets among common and preferred shareholders by modeling each class of stock as a call option with distinct claims on the company's assets.[3]

The AICPA Practice Aid, which was issued in 2004, provided a general summary of the then-current best valuation practices, and identified the OPM as one of the three primary allocation methods used to establish the value of the common and preferred stock for a privately held entity. While selection of an appropriate allocation methodology largely depends on the individual facts and circumstances for the company being valued, an improved understanding of the mechanics of the OPM has made it increasingly popular among practitioners due to the perceived "objectivity" of some of its key assumptions, such as risk-free rates, time frame to expected liquidity event, and to a lesser extent, volatility. (In contrast, the probability-weighted expected returns method, which can be thought of as a discrete version of the OPM, relies on a selection of exit scenario probabilities that are more subjective and lack the strict quantitative elements of the OPM.)

However, a thorough understanding of the inputs in the OPM is critical in order to avoid certain pitfalls in its application. As the Practice Aid states, the "method may be complex to implement and sensitive to certain key assumptions, such as the volatility assumption (one of the required inputs under the Black-Scholes model), that are not readily subject to contemporaneous or subsequent validation. Additionally, the lack of trading history for a privately held enterprise makes the subjectivity of the volatility assumption a potential limitation on the effectiveness of the method to determine fair value."[4]

MERTON'S MODEL—ASSET VS. EQUITY VOLATILITY

In Merton's model, the firm's capital structure consists of equity and a zero-coupon bond with a principal **P**. The principal is due at maturity time **T**, and the debt-holders have absolute priority claim on the firm's assets at maturity. The equity is then the residual claim on the firm's assets beyond the claim of the bondholders and can be represented with the following relationship.

Payoff

$$\text{Equity Payoff} = \text{Max}(A_T - P, 0)$$

where A_T is the firm asset value at maturity time **T**.
   P is the principal due to the bondholders at maturity.

In other words, if the firm asset value at maturity is below the principal due to the bondholders, the return to the equity holders is zero. However, if the firm asset value at maturity exceeds the principal that is due, the incremental upside beyond the principal threshold represents the return to the equity holders. The payoff to the equity holders is then identical to the payoff of a European call option on the firm's assets where strike price is set equal to the principal due to the bondholders and the expiration of the option is set equal to the maturity of the debt.

Assuming that the underlying asset value of the firm follows a stochastic process with constant drift and constant asset volatility σ_A, the call option that represents the firm's equity value can be priced using the standard Black-Scholes formula:

Black-Scholes Formula

$$\text{Equity Value} = \text{Call}(A_0, P, T)$$

$$\text{Call}(A_0, P, T) = A_0 * N(d_1) - P * e^{-rT} * N(d_2)$$

$$d_1 = \frac{Ln(A_0/P) + (r + \sigma_A^2/2)T}{\sigma_A\sqrt{T}}$$

$$d_2 = d_1 - \sigma_A\sqrt{T}$$

where A_0 is the firm asset value at time $t = 0$ (today).

   P is the principal due to the bondholders at maturity (the strike of the call).

   T is the time to maturity of the bond (the option's time to expiration).

   r is the continuously compounded risk-free interest rate.

   σ_A is the constant asset volatility of the firm.

Because the value of the equity is a call option on the firm's assets, the appropriate input in the foregoing Black-Scholes equation is the asset volatility σ_A. The asset volatility is generally unobservable. However, the equity volatility of the firm can be calculated directly from the standard deviation of the firm's stock price returns (assuming that the company is publicly traded, which is the case here). It would be inappropriate to input the observed equity volatility σ_E in the foregoing equation, because the firm's leverage affects the equity volatility. Consequently, the observed equity volatility can be different from the asset volatility. If one finds a mathematical relationship between the equity and asset volatilities of the firm, this relationship can be used to calculate the implied asset volatility from the observed equity volatility. The asset volatility can then be correctly used in Black-Scholes formula.

Because the value of the equity of the firm is directly related to the value of the firm's assets through the Black-Scholes formula as discussed previously, it is not surprising that a similarly direct relationship exists between the equity and asset volatilities of the firm. Merton shows[5] that the relationship is as follows.

Asset vs. Equity Volatility

$$\sigma_E = \Delta_E * (A_0/E_0) * \sigma_A = N(d_1) * (A_0/E_0) * \sigma_A$$

where A_0 is the firm asset value at time $t=0$ (today).

E_0 is the firm equity value at time $t=0$ (today).

$N(d_1)$ is a familiar term from the Black-Scholes formula and is also known as the call option's "delta" (a measure of the call's sensitivity with respect to changes in the underlying asset value).

σ_A is the asset volatility of the firm.

σ_E is the equity volatility of the firm.

Rearranging the foregoing expression, one obtains the corresponding inverse relationship.

Asset vs. Equity Volatility

$$\sigma_A = (1/\Delta_E) * (E_0/A_0) * \sigma_E = (1/N(d_1)) * (E_0/A_0) * \sigma_E$$

The application of this model is easily illustrated through an example. Assume the observable market cap of a public company is $50 million and the calculated equity volatility of the company is 70.0 percent. Further, assume that the company has issued a single zero-coupon bond with principal of $40 million that matures in two years and the current risk-free interest rate is 2.0 percent (for purposes of the model, a flat term structure is assumed).

Because the equity market capitalization of the firm is modeled as a call option on the assets, a Black-Scholes formula can be set up with the following inputs.

Example 1: Model Set-Up

A_0 (current firm asset value) = unknown
P (debt principal) = $40 million
T (time to maturity) = 2.0 years
r (risk-free interest rate) = 2.0%
σ_A (asset volatility) = unknown

The current value of the firm assets and the asset volatility are initially unknown. However, the result of the Black-Scholes formula represents the equity value of the firm and must agree with the observed market cap of $50 million. Furthermore, the observed equity volatility of the firm is 70.0 percent and it is related to the asset volatility through the formulas in Assets vs. Equity Volatility previously.

Example 1: Market Data

$$E_0 \text{ (current firm equity value)} = \$50 \text{ million}$$

$$\sigma_E \text{ (equity volatility)} = 70.0\%$$

Using the foregoing information with Excel's solver function, an iterative process can be used to obtain the implied current value of the firm assets $A_0 = \$87,138,636$ as well as the implied asset volatility $\sigma_A = 42.2$ percent. One can verify that these implied values are correct by plugging in the appropriate inputs into the Black-Scholes formula and observing that the output reconciles to the market cap equity as expected.

Example 1: Model Output

Inputs are as follows:

A_0 (current firm asset value) = $87,138,636

P (debt principal) = $40 million

T (time to maturity) = 2.0 years

r (risk-free interest rate) = 2.0%

σ_A (asset volatility) = 42.2%

Output is as follows:

$$\text{Call}(A_0, P, T) = \$50,000,000$$

$$\sigma_A = (1/N(d_1)) * (E_0/A_0) * \sigma_E = (1/\text{Normsdist}(1.6694)) *$$
$$(\$50,000,000/\$87,138,636) * 70\% = 42.2\%$$

Again, the correct input into the Black-Scholes formula is the asset volatility σ_A which in the foregoing example was shown to be 42.2 percent and is significantly different from the observed equity volatility of the firm $\sigma_E = 70.0$ percent. Furthermore, the relationship between the asset and equity volatility, expressed through the Black Scholes Formula earlier depends on the level of the firm's leverage through the term E_0/A_0. It also depends on the call option's delta $N(d_1)$, which in this case represents the sensitivity of the equity value (call option) with respect to changes in the asset value and can range from 0 to 1, depending on the "moneyness" of the call option. Finally, the Black-Scholes model assumes that the firm's asset volatility σ_A is constant whereas the equity volatility fluctuates as the call option's delta as well as the firm's leverage change. For this reason, the equity volatility here is often referred to as the "instantaneous equity volatility." In the foregoing example, we calibrated the model by reconciling the formulas to the observed instantaneous equity volatility of 70.0 percent as of the valuation date and were able to obtain the implied asset volatility of 42.2 percent, which, as already mentioned, is then assumed to be constant.

THE OPTION-PRICING METHOD

As mentioned earlier, the OPM is an extension of Merton's original model. The primary difference is that the firm's capital structure is modified to include convertible preferred stock. Much like the bondholders in Merton's model, the preferred shareholders have a priority claim on the firm's asset upon "maturity" (exit) through their liquidation preference. However, an added complexity is that the preferred stock may be convertible, which means that preferred shareholders can convert to common stock when such a conversion yields returns above the liquidation preference.

In the following example, there are 4,000,000 common shares and 1,000,000 preferred shares with a liquidation preference of $35 per share. The current aggregate equity value of the company that is to be allocated between the common and the preferred stockholders is $50,000,000. The expected time to a liquidity event is two years. The asset volatility is 50.0 percent, and the risk-free rate is 5.0 percent.

Example 2: Capitalization Table

Equity Class	Number of Shares	Liquidation per Share	Total Liquidation Preference
Series A Preferred	1,000,000	$35.00	$35,000,000
Common	4,000,000		
Total	5,000,000		$35,000,000

In this simple example, there are two "breakpoints"—$35,000,000 (the total liquidation preference of the preferred) and $175,000,000 (the point at which the preferred stockholders should convert to common). In the following table, the appropriate three call options are set up with strike prices set equal to the respective breakpoints.

Example 2: Black-Scholes ($\sigma_A = 50.0\%$)

	Breakpoint	$N(d_1)$	Call Value
Call 1	$ 0	1.0000	$50,000,000
Call 2	$ 35,000,000	0.8404	$22,537,208
Call 3	$175,000,000	0.1003	$ 1,290,568

Example 2: Allocation

	$N(d_1)$ Difference	Call Value Difference	Common %	Preferred %
Call 1–Call 2	0.1596	$27,462,792	0.0%	100.0%
Call 2–Call 3	0.7401	$21,246,640	100.0%	0.0%
Call 3	0.1003	$ 1,290,568	80.0%	20.0%
Total	1.0000	$50,000,000		

In order to arrive at the allocated value to the common shareholders, we calculate the differences in successive call option values and multiply this by the appropriate "participation" percentage for the common shareholders:

$$\text{Common Stock Value} = 0.0\% * \$27,462,792 + 100.0\% *$$
$$\$21,246,640 + 80\% * \$1,290,568$$
$$= \$22,279,095$$

Unlike Merton's model, where the common equity was a single call option on the firm's assets, here the common equity is represented as a portfolio of call options on the firm's assets (long and short calls with different strikes corresponding to the different breakpoints, as well as different weightings corresponding to the participation percentages for the common). The portfolio of options is necessary because the capital structure includes convertible preferred stock. The single call option in Merton's model, which represented the value of the common equity, is replaced by a linear combination of call options in the OPM.

Furthermore, recall that the exact relationship between the common equity volatility, and the asset volatility in Merton's model was given by the expression from Asset vs. Equity Volatility earlier:

$$\sigma_E = \Delta_E \,^* (A_0/E_0) \,^* \sigma_A$$

where the Δ_E is the "delta" factor which measures the sensitivity of the common equity value with respect to changes in the underlying asset value of the firm. For a simple European call option (which is the case in Merton's model), $\Delta = N(d_1)$ where $N(d_1)$ is a familiar expression from the Black-Scholes formula (the cumulative standard normal distribution evaluated at d_1).

The same relationship between the asset volatility and the common equity volatility holds in the OPM. However, since the common equity is a linear combination of call options, it can be shown that the corresponding "delta" factor for the common equity is a linear combination of the "deltas" for the individual calls:[6]

Common Stock Delta $(\Delta_E) = 0.0\% \,^* 0.1596 + 100.0\% \,^*$
$$0.7401 + 80.0\% \,^* 0.1003 = 0.8203$$

Note the similarities with the expression for the foregoing common stock value—the "weightings" or "participation percentages" that are applied are the same. Here, the call option value difference is substituted for the difference in the "deltas" for the individual calls. The "deltas" of the individual calls are the respective $N(d_1)$ factors present in the Black-Scholes formula.

We are now in a position to calculate the implied common equity volatility from the expression in Asset vs. Equity Volatility earlier. Recall that the asset volatility σ_A that is used in the example is 50.0 percent, the aggregate value of the firm's assets is $50,000,000, the common equity value is calculated to be $22,279,095, and the "delta" of the common equity is calculated to be 0.8203:

$$\sigma_E = \Delta_E * (A_0/E_0) * \sigma_A = 0.8203 * (\$50,000,000/\$22,279,095) * 50.0\%$$
$$= 92.1\%$$

This example illustrates that, given the assumed asset volatility of 50 percent, the implied common equity volatility is as high as 92 percent. It is not surprising that the volatility of the common stock is considerably higher than the overall asset volatility of the firm since the liquidation preferences of the preferred stock add a significant amount of leverage to the common equity investment.

We can now apply an identical calculation in order to find the implied volatility of the preferred stock:

$$\text{Preferred Stock Value} = 100.0\% * \$27,462,792 + 0.0\% * \$21,246,640$$
$$+ 20.0\% * \$1,290,568 = \$27,720,095$$
$$\text{Preferred Stock Delta } (\Delta_P) = 100.0\% * 0.1596 + 0.0\% * 0.7401$$
$$+ 20.0\% * 0.1003 = 0.1797$$
$$\sigma_P = \Delta_P * (A_0/P_0) * \sigma_A = 0.1797 * (\$50,000,000/$$
$$\$27,720,905) * 50.0\% = 16.2\%$$

Again, the implied preferred equity volatility is considerably lower than the common equity volatility and the aggregate volatility of the firm's assets as expected. The "debt-like" features of the preferred stock (the liquidation preference) provide the preferred stockholders with downside protection in the event of declines in the asset value of the firm. To the extent that volatility is a measure of risk, the relationship confirms that an investment in preferred stock of the company carries considerably less risk than a common equity investment in the same enterprise.

Also, the large difference between the implied volatilities for the preferred and common equity is a result of the leverage introduced by the preferred stock, which can be thought of as the level of "moneyness" of the common equity. Indeed, when the current asset value is \$50,000,000 as in the preceding example, given the liquidation breakpoint of \$35,000,000, the common stock is not very deep in-the-money. To express that quantitatively, the calculated value of the common equity accounts for only 44.6 percent of the total asset value, despite the fact that common equity shares account for 80.0 percent of the company shares on a fully diluted basis.

If the asset value of the firm is set to $500,000,000, all other assumptions are kept the same; the common equity will be deep in-the-money. Here, the value of the common equity implied from the OPM accounts for approximately 79.8 percent of the total asset value. The implied volatilities of the common and preferred equity ultimately converge to the asset volatility of 50 percent as the asset value increases. This relationship is illustrated in the following table.

Example 2: Common and Preferred Equity Volatilities as a Function of Asset Value

Beginning Firm Asset Value	Asset Volatility	Implied Preferred Equity Volatility	Implied Common Equity Volatility
$ 50,000,000	50.0%	16.2%	92.1%
$100,000,000	50.0%	15.0%	67.7%
$150,000,000	50.0%	24.3%	59.1%
$200,000,000	50.0%	32.9%	55.1%
$250,000,000	50.0%	38.8%	53.1%
$300,000,000	50.0%	42.7%	51.9%
$350,000,000	50.0%	45.1%	51.3%
$400,000,000	50.0%	46.7%	50.8%
$450,000,000	50.0%	47.7%	56.6%
$500,000,000	50.0%	48.4%	50.4%

An important point that we will revisit in a subsequent section is that, under the OPM, the asset volatility is assumed to be constant. The implied volatilities of the common and preferred stock, on the contrary, are non-constant and will fluctuate as different parameters of the model change, such as firm value, leverage, time frame to exit, or risk-free rate.

ASSET VOLATILITY SELECTION

As discussed earlier, the OPM views the common and preferred equity as contingent claims on the assets of the firm. In the Black-Scholes framework, these contingent claims can be priced using the Black-Scholes call option formula where one of the required inputs is the asset volatility of the firm.

Because the OPM deals with privately held businesses that have no trading history, neither the asset nor the equity volatility is directly observable.

In practice, the volatility of a private entity is estimated using a selection of publicly traded comparables. For instance, when pricing employee stock options for recognizing share-based compensation expenses under SFAS 123R, privately held entities typically estimate the expected volatility of their common stock by considering the historical and/or implied volatilities of similar entities whose shares are publicly traded:

> Observable Equity (Share) Volatility—Guideline Companies
> ↓
> Estimated Equity (Share) Volatility—Target Company

Practitioners have adopted a similar approach for estimating the volatility input in the OPM and rely on a comparative analysis using a selected pool of guideline public companies. A subtlety that is often overlooked, however, is that the required volatility input in the OPM is the firm's asset volatility. Whereas an employee stock option is a call on the firm's common equity, it seems only natural to look at the common equity volatilities of the comparable public companies in order to get an estimate for the common equity volatility of the target. In contrast, under the OPM, call options are priced on the firm's assets. In order to estimate the asset volatility input, one needs to measure the asset volatilities of the guideline public companies.

> Unobservable Asset Volatility—Guideline Companies
> ↓
> Estimated Asset Volatility—Target Company

Asset volatility is unobservable even for public companies. Faced with that problem, practitioners often use equity volatilities of the guideline public companies as a proxy for the asset volatility assumption of the OPM. The asset and equity volatilities of an early stage enterprise are not the same, due to the leverage introduced by the preferred equity.

This mixing of "apples and oranges" can result in significant mispricings. Very often, the volatility input used in the OPM is also used in the Black-Scholes formula to calculate the employee compensation expense under SFAS 123R. Using the earlier example where the asset volatility of 50 percent of a particular early stage company resulted in an implied common equity volatility of 92 percent, the impact on the value of a call option can be shown. An at-the-money five-year $10 call option is worth $4.96

when the risk-free rate and volatility are 5 percent and 50 percent, respectively. The value of the call option increases to $7.33 when the volatility rises to 92 percent.

Although asset volatilities of public companies are unobservable, their equity volatilities are observable. Hence, one way to address the issue is to "unlever" the observed equity volatilities of the public guideline companies, estimate their implied asset volatilities, and use that as a proxy for the asset volatility of the target:

Observable Equity (Share) Volatility—Guideline Companies →Implied Asset Volatility—Guideline Companies
↓
Estimated Asset Volatility—Target Company

Unfortunately, a general relationship between the asset and equity volatilities of the guideline companies may be hard or impossible to find, at least from a practical standpoint. Recall that Merton found a direct relationship between the asset and equity volatilities of a firm with a simple capital structure consisting of a single zero-coupon bond and equity. Introducing bonds with periodic interest payments, different maturities or embedded call, put or conversion features into the capital structure of the company makes the analysis increasingly more complex. Large publicly traded entities may have a complex structure of liabilities that includes fixed- and floating-rate debt issuances with various levels of seniority, maturities, and embedded derivatives. These intricate capital structures do not fit into the simple financing decision model assumed in Merton's framework, and modeling the relationship between the asset and equity volatilities of a public entity is beyond the scope of this article.

However, modeling the relationship between asset and common equity volatility for a venture-stage private entity financed by preferred and common stock issuances is a straightforward extension of Merton's original model, as demonstrated earlier. While an entity may have different classes of preferred stock in its capital structure, they all have the same "maturity" (i.e., the expected time frame to a liquidity event). Furthermore, the preferred stock of early stage companies resembles zero-coupon debt since it does not pay periodic cash dividends (if there are any cumulative dividends, they are typically accrued to the liquidation preference and distributed at the time of the assumed exit event). Therefore, we could match the observed equity volatility of the guideline public companies with the equity volatility of the target (consistent with the approach used under SFAS 123R), and then use the relationship between the equity and asset volatilities of the target to obtain the implied asset volatility of the target, a required input into the OPM.

Observable Equity (Share) Volatility—Guideline Companies
↓
Estimated Equity Volatility—Target Company

Implied Asset Volatility—Target Company

Let us illustrate this approach with an example.

Example 3: Capitalization Table

Equity Class	Number of Shares	Liquidation per Share	Total Liquidation Preference
Series A Preferred	1,000,000	$35.00	$35,000,000
Common	4,000,000		
Total	5,000,000		$35,000,000

There are 4,000,000 common shares and 1,000,000 preferred shares with a liquidation preference of $35 per share. The current aggregate equity value of the company that needs to be allocated among the common and the preferred is $50,000,000. The expected time frame to liquidity is two years and the risk-free rate is 5.0 percent. Previously, we had stated an assumed asset volatility of 50.0 percent without making any reference to the source or explaining how this was selected. Now let us assume that we have identified a pool of comparable public companies and have determined that based on the historical and/or implied stock price volatilities of these benchmark companies, the appropriate equity volatility of the target company is 70.0 percent. We then use the relationship between the equity and asset volatilities of the target to find that the implied asset volatility for our company is 30.5 percent. Note that the relationship is circular since, in order to determine the implied asset volatility, we need the fair value of the common equity as well as the "delta" of the common equity. On the other hand, we need the asset volatility in order to find the fair value of the common equity, and the "delta." This circular relationship is easily handled by the "goal-seek" function in Excel, which solves for the asset volatility that is needed in order for the model to reconcile to the estimated equity volatility of 70.0 percent.

Example 3: Black-Scholes ($\sigma_A = 30.5\%$)

	Breakpoint	$N(d_1)$	Call Value
Call 1	$ 0	1.0000	$50,000,000
Call 2	$ 35,000,000	0.8979	$19,524,499
Call 3	$175,000,000	0.0069	$ 42,583

Example 3: Allocation

$N(d_1)$ difference	Call Value Difference	Common %	Preferred %
Call 1–Call 2	0.1021	$30,475,501	0.0%	100.0%
Call 2–Call 3	0.8910	$19,481,915	100.0%	0.0%
Call 3	0.0069	$ 42,583	80.0%	20.0%
Total	1.0000	$50,000,000		

$$\text{Common Stock Value} = 0.0\% * \$30,475,501 + 100.0\% * \$19,481,915$$
$$+ 80\% * \$42,583 = \$19,515,982$$

$$\text{Common Stock Value per Share} = \$19,515,982/4,000,000 = \$4.88$$

We can also verify that the model is properly calibrated by checking that the asset volatility σ_A of 30.5 percent corresponds to an equity volatility of 70.0 percent, in agreement with the selection from the guideline companies:

$$\text{Common Stock Delta } (\Delta_E) = 0.0\% * 0.1021 + 100.0\% * 0.8910$$
$$+ 80.0\% * 0.0069 = 0.8965$$
$$\sigma_A = (1/\Delta_E) * (E_0/A_0) * \sigma_E = (1/0.8965) *$$
$$(\$19{,}515{,}982/\$50{,}000{,}000) * 70.0\%$$
$$= 30.5\%$$

It is worth making a point that, if we had taken the estimated equity volatility of 70.0 percent from the guideline companies and used that directly as an asset volatility input into the OPM without any adjustments for leverage, we would have obtained very different results. One can easily verify that keeping all other inputs the same and changing the volatility input in the OPM from 30.5 percent to 70.0 percent, the resulting common equity value per share would be $6.28, an overestimation by approximately 29 percent.

CONCLUSION

Although somewhat esoteric, the foregoing discussion addresses an often-overlooked application of volatility in the OPM when it is used to allocate a company's overall equity value between different classes of stock that arguably have different volatilities. The examples, buttressed by detailed narrative, attempt to demonstrate a fairly easy methodology to account for differences in volatility among various asset classes. More sophisticated binomial models can be built that allow for single-input volatility. See Chapter 7 for a more complete discussion of advanced valuation techniques using binomial models.

Derivation of Asset and Equity Volatility in the Merton Model

An outline of the derivation of the relationship between asset and equity volatility, as presented in Merton's original work, is sketched as follows. Assume that the assets of the firm **A** follow a geometric Brownian motion satisfying the following stochastic differential equation:

$$dA = (\mu_A * A)dt + (\sigma_A * A)dW \qquad (A.1)$$

where

  μ_A is the instantaneous "drift" of the asset price process.

  σ_A is the instantaneous asset volatility.

  dW is a Wiener process.

Suppose that the equity of the firm E satisfies the stochastic price process that follows:

$$dE = (\mu_E * E)dt + (\sigma_E * E)dW_E \qquad (A.2)$$

where

  μ_E is the instantaneous "drift" of the equity price process.

  σ_E is the instantaneous equity volatility.

  dW_E is a Wiener process.

If we assume that the equity of the firm at any point of time can be written as a function of the assets of the firm and time using the functional relationship $E = F(A, t)$, we can use Ito's lemma to express the dynamics of E in the following manner:

$$
\begin{aligned}
dE &= dF = F_t dt + F_A dA + (1/2) * F_{AA}(dA)^2 \\
&= F_t dt + F_A * [(\mu_A * A)dt + (\sigma_A * A)dW] + (1/2) * F_{AA}[(\sigma_A^2 * A^2)dt] \\
&= [F_t + F_A * \mu_A * A + (1/2) * F_{AA} * \sigma_A^2 * A^2]dt + [F_A * \sigma_A * A]dW
\end{aligned}
$$

$$(A.3)$$

where the partial derivatives are given with the notation $F_t = \partial F/\partial t$, $F_A = \partial F/\partial A$ and $F_{AA} = \partial^2 F/\partial A^2$. Setting the like terms in (A.2) and (A.3) equal to each other, one obtains the following relationships:

$$F_t + F_A * \mu_A * A + (1/2) * F_{AA} * \sigma_A^2 * A^2 \equiv \mu_E * E \qquad (A.4a)$$

$$F_A * \sigma_A * A \equiv \sigma_E * E \qquad (A.4b)$$

$$dW \equiv dW_E \qquad (A.4c)$$

In particular, (A.4b) shows the relationship between the instantaneous asset volatility σ_A, and the instantaneous equity volatility σ_E, which can re-written as $\sigma_E = F_A * (A/E) * \sigma_A$, where $F_A = \partial F/\partial A$.

In Merton's simple framework, the equity is a European call option on the assets of the firm. Therefore the functional expression that relates the equity value to the firm assets is given by $E = F(A, t) = \text{Call}(A, T, \sigma_A)$. In the Black-Scholes setting, $F_A = \Delta_E$ where for a European call option, the "option" delta is given by the expression $\Delta_E = N(d_1)$.

In the framework of the OPM, the equity is a linear combination of call options on the assets of the firm. Therefore the functional expression that relates the common equity value to the firm assets is given by

$$E = F(A, t) = w_1 * \text{Call}_1 + w_2 * \text{Call}_2 + \ldots + w_k * \text{Call}_k$$

where

$w_1, w_2, \ldots, w_k$ represent the (signed) weightings of the different calls (i.e. the "participation percentages").

$\text{Call}_1, \text{Call}_2, \ldots, \text{Call}_k$ represent call options on the firm assets with different strikes (corresponding to the different breakpoints).

In the Black-Scholes setting, the "delta" of equity is given by the linear combination of the "deltas" of the individual calls in the portfolio $F_A = w_1 * \Delta_1 + w_2 * \Delta_2 + \ldots + w_k * \Delta_k$, where for any call option Call_m in the portfolio, the delta of that call is given by $\Delta_m = N(d_1)_m$

REFERENCES

1. American Institute of Certified Public Accountants. (2004). *Valuation of Privately-held-company Equity Securities issued as Compensation.* Practice Aid. New York: Task Force of the AICPA.
2. Merton, R. (1974). "On the pricing of corporate debt: the risk structure of interest rates." *Journal of Finance* 29(2), 449–470.
3. Hull, J., Nelken, I., and White, A. (2004). "Merton's model, credit risk and volatility skews." *Journal of Credit Risk* 1(1), 3–28.
4. Crosbie, P. and Bohn, J. (2003). Modeling default risk. Working paper retrieved from http://www.moodyskmv.com/research/singleObligor_wp.html.

5. Jones, E., Mason, S., and Rosenfeld, E. (1984). "Contingent claims analysis of corporate capital structures: an empirical investigation." *Journal of Finance* 39(3), 611–625.
6. Elizalde, A. (2005). "Credit risk models II: structural models." Working paper retrieved from http://www.abelelizalde.com/.

Notes

CHAPTER 2 Understanding Early Stage Preferred Stock Rights

1. National Venture Capital Association. http://www.nvca.org/pdf/Q2_08_Exits_Release.pdf.
2. Dow Jones Venture Capital Deal Terms Report, November 2008, Dow Jones & Company, Inc.

CHAPTER 3 Enterprise Valuation Approaches

1. Final Regs, 409A, paragraph 4(c)i.

CHAPTER 4 Application of the Option-Pricing Method in Allocating Enterprise Value

1. Source: Thompson Financial Data *VentureExpert* database.
2. See Grabowski, Roger J., "Cost of Capital Estimation in the Current Distressed Environment," *Journal of Applied Research in Accounting and Finance*, Vol. 4, No. 1, pp. 31–40, 2009.

CHAPTER 5 Application of the Probability-Weighted Expected Returns Method in Allocating Enterprise Value

1. Updated U.S. Private Equity Valuation Guidelines, March 2007. Available at www.peigg.org/images/2007_March_Updated_US_PE_Valuation_Guidelines.pdf.
2. "Private Equity Returns: An Empirical Examination of the Exit of Venture-backed Companies," Sanjiv R. Das, Murali Jagannathan, and Atulya Sarin, *Journal of Investment Management*, Vol. 1, No. 1 (2003).
3. In practice, I have encountered resistance in audit reviews to my use of discounts for lack of control (DLOC). The rationale for their refusal of a DLOC is a 2004 SEC speech by Todd Hardiman, which I have found to be misinterpreted and misunderstood. I cover this topic in more detail in Chapter 6, so for purposes of this PWERM, I ignore this discussion and resistance.
4. The weighted average strike price of the granted options was $0.60.
5. For purposes of this example, transaction costs associated with a sale or IPO were not considered. Depending on the facts and circumstances of the engagement, these costs may need to be taken into account.
6. The per-share value has been determined using the same discount rates used to discount the common stock. This is typical, as it can be difficult to quantify the risk adjustment between the common and preferred stock.

CHAPTER 6 Applicable Discounts for Early Stage Companies

1. Business Valuation Resources, LLP.
2. Speech by SEC Staff at 32nd AICPA National Conference on Current SEC and PCAOB Developments, by Todd E. Hardiman, December 6, 2004.
3. IRS Section 409A regulations.
4. Francis A. Longstaff "How Much Can Marketability Affect Security Values?" *Journal of Finance*, Vol. l, No. 5. December 1995.
5. John D. Finnerty, "The Impact of Transfer Restrictions on Stock Prices," white paper, Fordham University, June 2003.
6. Sanjiv Das, Murali Jagannathan, and Atulya Sarin, "Private Equity Returns: An Empirical Examination of the Exit of Venture-Backed Companies," *Journal of Investment Management*, Vol. 1, No. 1 (2003).

CHAPTER 7 Advanced Valuation Topics for Early Stage Companies

1. Copeland, Tom, *Options, Futures and Other Derivatives* and Vladimir Antikarov, *Real Options, Revised Edition: A Practitioner's Guide*.
2. This concept was illustrated by David C. Dufendach in "Calculating the Effect of Anticipated Dilution on the Value of New Ventures: A Real Options Approach," *Valuation Strategies*, Jan–Feb 2003.
3. This example is adapted from David C. Dufendach, "Combining Valuation and Allocation in a Single Model: An Extension of the Option Pricing Method," *Valuation Strategies*, 2009.
4. This is the assumption here; one could also assume a small liquidation value if the financing is not obtained.
5. Plummer, James L., *QED Report on Venture Capital Financial Analysis*, Palo Alto: QED Research, Inc., 1987.
6. Scherlis, Daniel R. and William A. Sahlman, "A Method for Valuing High-Risk, Long Term, Investments: The Venture Capital Method," *Harvard Business School Teaching Note 9-288-006*, Boston: Harvard Business School Publishing, 1989.
7. Babson College, William D. Bygrave, June 1997, "Classic Venture Capital in the Next Millennium".

APPENDIX A

1. Enterprise value is typically defined as equity plus debt.
2. Although these three methods do not comprise the only methods for performing equity allocation analyses, they have been widely used as generally accepted methods for determining equity allocation for tax compliance and financial reporting purposes.
3. If the strike price is set equal to zero, the Black-Scholes formula doesn't work. For this reason, practitioners generally use a number close to zero (such as $0.001) for the strike price.
4. This analysis assumes that no dividends would be declared or accrued. Declared or accrued dividends may be added to the liquidation preference to determine the appropriate exercise price(s), depending on the characteristics of the preferred shares.
5. Commonly referred to as a compound option.

6. For example, a typical assumption is to assume the common stock options behave as European call options (options that are not exercisable until the anticipated liquidation event). This allows us to use a closed form model, such as the Black-Scholes model, to determine call option values. This article also assumes no transaction costs for exercising an option.
7. Assuming a simple capital structure, where preferred does not participate or is convertible.
8. The Treasury stock technique assumes that in-the-money options as of the valuation date are converted to common shares on the valuation date based on the exchange of exercise proceeds for common shares at the current common share price. A second technique would assume that in-the-money options are immediately exercised as of the valuation date, converting to common one to one regardless of the current stock price. Both of these methods treat out-of-the-money options as if they have no impact on the underlying common stock price.
9. Note that the net value of common equity per share at $2.00 is confirmed by dividing $300 ($250 in additional value plus $50 of prior value) by a total of 150 shares (100 original common and 50 from option exercise).

APPENDIX B

1. Merton, R. (1974). On the pricing of corporate debt: the risk structure of interest rates. *Journal of Finance* 29(2), 449–470.
2. Crosbie, P. and Bohn, J. (2003). Modeling default risk. Working paper retrieved from http://www.moodyskmv.com/research/singleObligor_wp.html, accessed 18 April 2009.
3. American Institute of Certified Public Accountants. (2004). *Valuation of privately-held-company equity securities issued as compensation*. Practice Aid. New York: Task Force of the AICPA.
4. Paragraph 148, Practice Aid.
5. See Derivation of Asset and Equity Volatility in the "Merton" Model at the end of this Appendix for an outline of the derivation.
6. See Derivation of Asset and Equity Volatility in the "Merton" Model at end of this Appendix.

Index

A

Advanced valuation. *See also* Valuation
  allocating residual value, 131, 133–137
  compound option in, 126, 127–131, 137–139
  executive stock compensation in, 143
  overview of, 125–127
  sequential option in, 127–131
  utilizing OPM as, 127
  venture capital rates of return in, 139–143

AICPA, 9, 35

AICPA Practice Aid:
  application of market approach, 45
  description of cost approach, 40
  rates of return for venture capital funds studies, 139
  stages of development in, 52
  Valuation of Private Equity Securities Issued in Other Than a Business Combination, 50
  Valuation of Privately-Held-Company Equity Securities Issued as Compensation, 145, 155
  valuation practices, 156

Allocation method. *See* Probability-weighted expected returns method (PWERM)

Amazon.com, 8

American Institute of Certified Public Accountants (AICPA). *See* AICPA

Angelesoft.net, 53, 110

Angel investors, 54

Antidilution rights, 25–26

Appraisers, 40, 55, 90

Articles of Incorporation, 63, 68–69

Asian put option, 118

Asset-based approach. *See* Cost approach

Asset value:
  post-money, 115
  underlying, 62–63
  volatility and, 61

Asset volatility:
  derivation in Merton model, 170–172
  selection of, 165–170

Asset *vs.* equity volatility, 157–161

ATM call, 115, 116

At-the-money call option, 115, 116

At-the-money put option, 115, 116

Audit and Accounting Practice Aid Series, 35

Printed and bound by CPI Group (UK) Ltd, Croydon, CR0 4YY

24/04/2025

14661392-0001